The Gospel
for the Privileged

Comments, criticisms, questions, or anything of the sort can be sent to gospelfortheprivileged@gmail.com

Endorsements: If you would like to write an endorsement that may be included in future editions of this book, I would greatly appreciate that. Send them to gospelfortheprivileged@gmail.com

Reviews: If you would like to support this work, please leave an honest review on Amazon and share this work with your friends who you think might possibly benefit from it.

Social Media: You can stay up to date by finding @gospelfortheprivileged on instagram.

Cover Design: Ridge Rhine (Instagram: @ridgerhine)
Proofreading and extensive input from: Abigail Rhine, Joshua Columbus, and Juliana Olson.

ISBN: 9798713841089
Imprint: Independently published

Biography

My name is Nehemiah Olson. I'm just your average American Christian trying to live a faithful life in the midst of a "privileged" society. I am the "homeschooled son of a pastor" who grew up in various churches from Arizona to Illinois to Minnesota. Growing up in churches put me intimately ingrained in church life – exposing me the good, bad, and the hideous. I grew up primarily in the Evangelical Covenant Church but have increasingly come to consider myself a spiritual mut – someone who's faith has been influenced by a variety of traditions and who doesn't feel exactly at home in any specific one of them. I am also a former YWAMer having served in Australia and Papua New Guinea. I am a psychology graduate from the University of Minnesota Duluth and I currently reside in British Columbia, Canada where I live with my wife Juliana (whom I met while with YWAM).

Me too!

I accidently became a "writer" when the questions I had been wrestling with since my church saturated youth reached a breaking point and I had to process them somehow; so, I sat down and started writing until, to my surprise, I had written enough content for a book. I shared my writing with a few friends and, after much encouragement and convincing, I organized and refined my writing a bit and decided to share my inner world. So, thank you for joining me on this journey. I pray that this work will be a blessing and an encouragement to you.

ACKNOWLEDGEMENTS

First off, thank you for picking up this book. It means a lot.

And, I must acknowledge all those who helped make this book happen... too many to count. In all honesty, anyone who has influenced me in my faith journey has probably played a role in inspiring this book.

My wife Juliana who has walked with me and struggled through many of these issues with me, put up with my obsessive perfectionism, and has constantly provided me with feedback.

The 2016 YWAM Townsville family.
The UMD Intervarsity community.
The young adults at The Life Centre Mennonite Brethren church.
My family: brothers and sisters, mothers and fathers, and in-laws. These are the communities that have enabled and encouraged me to keep wrestling with God, his church, and myself. These are the people that have had the deepest impact on my life and faith.

Special thanks to Robert, Max, Bo, Tyson, Ben, Samo, Taylor, Jeff, Jeanine, Micaela, Gord, Monica, Mom, Dad, Jonny, Josh, Abby, Alethia, Ezra, Nathanael and Juliana (again) for your inspiration, friendship, encouragement, and loving-kindness.

Jesus, my love and my life. So gracious, so kind, so patient, so humble. What a privilege it is to serve you.

To
the poor,
the grief-ridden,
the humble,
the hungry and thirsty,
the merciful,
the pure in heart,
the peace makers,
and
the persecuted.

May I one day be as blessed as you.

CONTENTS

PROLOGUE

Why I Write

For much of my life I have wrestled with what it means to be a Christian living a comfortable life in America. For some reason, Christianity, as practiced by the Western church, never has sat right with me; I've always felt we were missing something. I grew up in the church, surrounded by many people with sincere and genuine love for Christ, among many more who did not have such sincerities. Even so, I always felt like there was *more* to the Christian life. I couldn't buy into the "contentment," "satisfaction," or, maybe more accurately, the *complacency* which saturated the culture of Christianity around me. What I read in the Bible, and even what I heard on Sunday morning, didn't line up with what I saw in the church.

In a most simplistic summary, the writings of Paul talk with much urgency and passion; the *Acts of the Apostle*s were filled with radical, Spirit-led lives; Jesus lived a life of simplicity and sacrifice; the prophets proclaimed a message of concern for the poor and repentance from arrogant lifestyles; and, the Psalmist prayed such desperate and honest prayers that it would be awkward and insincere if read in most of our churches. It seems that this urgent, passionate, Spirit-led, simplistic, sacrificial, compassionate, and humble message hasn't translated into lives that are defined by these biblical characteristics. Instead, I see, for the most part, people with comfortable jobs, nice families, nice houses, nice educations, and overall nice lives – lives that look little different than those of non-Christians except they may go to church once or twice a week, try not to sin, don't swear, try to live integrous lives, and occasionally go out of their way to love people (but I guess those characteristics can be found in the secular world as well!). But, what bothers me more than anything is that I, myself, have had difficulty seeing how my "Jesus-transformed life" is much different than most others in the world.

If my own failures aren't enough to disenfranchise me from Christ, the inadequacies and failures of the church could almost push me over the edge. In fact, the place I have most doubted Jesus and his saving power has been in the pew at the weekly church service! Let me explain: Throughout the week I read about the inspiring life of the early Christians in *Acts*, the beautiful life Jesus calls us to, and the letters of Paul that speak with authority and power; and after all this reading, I walk into the church and sometimes my faith feels weaker than it ever did throughout the week because I do not see the Spirit-filled Christlikeness or witness the power that I read about in scripture. Instead, I have seen churches embroiled in divisiveness, political opinions, hateful attitudes, meaningless debates, and deep concern for their own comfort. I was even in close proximity to a church that almost split on account of which color the carpet should be! *I mean, if these people really had the Spirit of God in them, wouldn't they be a lot different?* And, *if I really had the Spirit of God in me, wouldn't I be a lot different?*

I love Jesus and I love the church, but things usually don't seem to line up like they should. I often find it too easy to blame the church for such inconsistency. But the truth is that the church is made up of people like me and you; so, I think it's safe to say that such blame falls on me and you. Therefore, our duty as Christians must be to seek to resolve the deficiencies in our Christlikeness instead of passively receiving the complacent church that we have inherited.

Spiritual Dissonance

The inconsistency between what I read in the Bible and what I see in Christian practice (personally and in my church community) has created in me a sort of "spiritual dissonance." This spiritual dissonance is a sort of spiritual dissatisfaction, confusion, and discontentment that results from belonging to a church family whose reality vastly differs from its calling. It is the discomfort one experiences when the reality doesn't line up with the Christlike ideal. This could also be called a sort of "righteous indignation" at the injustice that the church does to the image of God. Yet, I cannot completely say that I am always "righteous" in my indignation, for I am a part of that very church that fills me with frustration. What's more, I myself possess much worldly cynicism as well. Even so, I pray that the discontentment I feel will motivate me unto a more transformed life.

I feel that the church too often discourages dwelling on such dissonance, citing that the Christian is expected to *always be satisfied* or is to already "have all the answers" (and if one doesn't have the answers, they can trust a pastor to give the answers). In my view, these are weak excuses for complacency or for not having to do the hard work of living a thoughtful Christian life. The truth is that not all the answers are easily found or even answered by the Christian faith. Others may brush such ramblings off as mere idealism or as holding to unrealistically high standards. Yet, *was not Jesus the very definition of an idealist?* (i.e., "be perfect as I am perfect"[1]).

In Jesus, the ideal becomes the reality. Because of this, I am convinced that this spiritual dissonance is not something that one should ignore or brush off, but it is something that one needs to wrestle with; lest one may lose their ability to spiritually discern anything and completely become out of touch with Christ. This entails a certain amount of wrestling with both God and the church. But wait, *isn't wrestling with God a bad idea?* No, I think that is precisely what it means to be in relationship with God. God renamed Jacob "Israel" to set him apart as "one who wrestles with God." Therefore, God's people, the Israelites, were defined as "those who wrestle with God." If we, too, are to enter into the new-covenantal relationship as God's people, does this not also entail that our relationship with God is marked by a little bit of wrestling? To wrestle with God, while maintaining deep trust in God's loving character will certainly bear a deep, blessed, and fruitful life. This book is my wrestling, and, in God's grace, this wrestling may bring us face to face with him.[2] *

I agree!

———————————————

*Wrestling is also messy, so I do not expect this book to be without mistakes or flaws. That's why wrestling is best done in community and with the input and accountability of others. Wrestling is also a continuous process. All the while, a book, by definition, is a static document. Therefore, I am sure I will one day look back on some of the things that I have written in here and think differently about them. Therefore, I am not asking you, as the reader, to simply agree with everything I say, but to wrestle alongside and with me.

The Narrow Path

It may be helpful if I give a tangible example of how this spiritual dissonance has appeared in my life. As a "young person," I have often longed to have an older mentor in the Christian faith who had spent their life fighting the good fight and is still fighting it. I looked and (probably in part due to my cynicism) I couldn't really find any. I longed to know those who had risked all for Christ – but the only ones I seemed to find were those who had left my part of the world to work as missionaries. I longed to find those who trusted God with their life, but I found those who worried more about their retirement funds than those who are going to hell or living in hell on earth. My hope is that I will trust God more every year than I did the last, but what I found were those who seemed to trust God less every year they got older. I hope to be more kind and sacrificially loving every year but what I found were those who got more stubborn and comfortable every year they got older. I saw retired people who spent most of their days golfing, vacationing, or spoiling their grandchildren – all the while thinking they deserved to live out their last days in comfort because they had "paid their dues" and now "it was the next generations turn."

I know that I am overgeneralizing a bit, but please bear with me. It was this same generation that disliked any changes that occurred in the church – even changes promoting church growth because they liked their small "close-knit community." It is this generation that resisted any change that would make them uncomfortable even though it would result in changed lives, new believers, and new ministry opportunities. It is this generation that resisted giving the next generation a turn because they didn't want to doctor the needs of the sick but wanted to

I was lucky enough to have one for awhile.

It is only loving "this generation" AND prayer – that will change things...

Many youth models used "entertainment" as the draw...

focus on the healthy. It was this generation that saw young people as people to entertain* (along with entertaining themselves) instead of adopting their passion and energy for the sake of the kingdom.

I admit that my generation's spiritual problems cannot be wholly pinned on the previous generation's failures. The blame probably falls more on an unavoidable historical period and a geographical place that has experienced a prosperity unparalleled throughout history. As our wealth has increased, it is no surprise that the call of Jesus has become apparently irrelevant and unpracticed. For, *it is harder for a camel to go through the eye of a needle than it is for a rich man to enter heaven.*[3] Such prosperity has bred comfortable complacency and increased in each subsequent generation that has failed to deal with prosperity the way Jesus did. In a way, we and the previous generation are simply the product of our prosperous times (but, I don't think we'll be able to use that excuse when we come face to face with Jesus).

As a result of such times, I see my generation starved of the gospel Jesus preached. Generally, this results in either (1) young people rejecting the church because the world has a more promising movement to be involved in, or (2) they end up accepting this complacent Christianity and living the comfortable lives as those before them did, or (3) they feel they do not belong to the church but still love Jesus and cannot leave the church. This third place is a hard place to

---

* If the church thinks they can attract and captivate young people through entertainment, they are deceived; for the world can entertain much better than the church. And even if a few young people end up being attracted by entertainment, they will grow up one day and realize the shallowness of what was offered to them. The draw of the gospel is the radical, beautiful, transformative, life and breath of Jesus.

be in, and as a result, many in this third place end up reverting to one of the other: being engaged in the world without Jesus or succumbing to a complacent life "with" Jesus.

I am trying to belong to that third group of people - I love Christ with all my heart and, because of this, I cannot leave the church as much as I am discouraged by it. The place that I am in is an awkward place to be in. It is a place where mainstream Western Christianity sees me as a "liberal progressive" while liberal progressives see me as a "conservative" Christian. Further, at times I find myself getting sucked into complacency, while at other times I find myself looking for hope in the social movements occurring outside the church. But the reality that I come back to is that *Jesus and his kingdom are the hope for this world,* and I must stay on the "narrow path" even though people on the left *and* the right see me as foolish.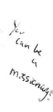

On this *foolish,* narrow path we are destined to find Jesus leading the way. For, Jesus himself rarely, if ever, "took sides" and was, in fact, rejected by those on all sides. Simplistically: the nationalistic, Jewish zealots rejected Christ for not being "radical" or violent enough; the right-wing Pharisees rejected Christ for not being holy enough; the Roman-sympathizing Sadducees rejected Jesus for being too radical; and the ruling Romans rejected Jesus almost out of mere indifference. There was not a political box for Jesus to place himself in or endorse. In actuality, Jesus was, at least in part, rejected and crucified for refusing to take sides with any major group of his day; and, to be certain, the only side he ever seemed to take was the side of the poor, sick, hungry, vulnerable, and politically powerless. Jesus was deeply "apolitical" for his time in that he did not conform to any preconceived political positions. This made him a profound political threat to the politics of his day. His politics were that of a "kingdom not of this world." In the same way, if we loosen ourselves from the grip of political zeitgeist and simply join Jesus on the narrow path, we may see his kingdom breaking in throughout all areas of society, political and otherwise – though, reader be warned, this may come at the cost of our own rejection and crucifixion. Yet, is that not the Christian life? *To pick up our cross and follow him.*

Disclaimer

I know some of what I have written might be out of cynicism, but I hope my cynicism doesn't smother my love for Christ as well as my brothers and sisters. I hope to get less cynical every year, and fuller of the radical love of Christ that doesn't notice what's wrong as much as I notice what is right and beautiful. Currently, I am cynical of the state of the church, but I am also extremely hopeful. All the while, I pray that my cynicism turns to godly discernment founded in the Spirit and that my cynicism will be swallowed up with childlike faith as I become more like Christ.

This book stems from my cynicism and my hope to move beyond cynicism while moving into the kind of life God calls us to. This is a challenge to the reader as well as an encouragement. But most of all, it is a conversation.

How I Write

First, I would like to note that you will probably notice many grammatical mistakes throughout, as I have not had the privilege of having an editor go through this book. That being said, I am trusting you as the reader to be able to be engaged with the book enough to notice when something doesn't make sense. And when something does not make sense, feel free to wrestle with it for a bit if it seems important, or just move on to the next sentence without letting it distract you very much. I preemptively thank you for your grace in this area. Additionally, I acknowledge that I will repeat myself many times throughout this book – possibly, a little too much. But, in each repetition, take it as your queue to allow the words to more fully penetrate your mind with each additional emphasis. For, repetition is a form a meditation that helps us build stronger pathways in our minds.

For clarity's sake, I would like to provide a little note on the formatting used throughout this book and instructions for the reader. First, every reference I make is marked by a little subscript that can be found in the reference section in the back of this book. These notes are not mandatory for understanding the book but may clarify where quotations or where statistics and various ideas came from. I have decided not to include scripture references within the text of the book, but these can be found by following the respective subscript. Furthermore, I have taken the liberty to paraphrase verses and when this happens the verse appears in italics followed by a subscript referencing the passage and translation used (if applicable).

I would leave out the
Disclaimer &
How I write ...

What I Write

To Whom I Write

Before I go any further, I wish to clarify the context in which this book is written and whom this book is intended to address. Throughout the book I make many references to the West, Western Christianity, White Christianity, American Christianity, North American Christianity, and similar combinations of words – I have chosen to sum all these up in the broad term, "privileged Christianity." Furthermore, anytime I use the words privileged Christian, you can assume I am talking about whatever definition of privilege that applies to you – whether that be White, American, Western, or, the such. This was written with a focus on the church in America and Canada but can still be applicable to anyone who has any unique privileges.

In our culture, "privilege" could be considered a controversial term, and if one is labelled as "having privilege" it can feel like one is being attacked. To those who resent being considered "privileged," I humbly ask you to look at your life situation and consider what you have that others don't, regardless of where it came from. The oft cited definition of *highest privilege* is summed up in the words "Christian, White, male, straight, educated, and rich." In this book, "privilege" is simply anything in your life that has given you an advantage over others and allows you to live a more comfortable life than others. "Privilege" also refers to the collective position of the Western church. For, anyone who even possesses an American, Canadian, European, or Australian passport is more materially and socially privileged than much of the world.

This book intends to challenge the thinking that has pervaded much of the privileged church's culture in these areas, while encouraging the church to take hold of the specific gifts and responsibilities God has given the privileged church in this very time.

To Whom I Do Not Write

Almost everyone is privileged in one way or another, therefore this book will be applicable to almost anyone who is willing to humbly consider how their privilege may be used for God's kingdom. Even so, I must say that this book is not necessarily for those who are *underprivileged*. It is also not intended to directly address areas in one's life that one does not have privilege. Therefore, my exhortations (particularly those in Chapter 3) to sacrifice, humility, suffering, etcetera, may not be directly applicable for certain individuals' situations. For example, this book is not meant to address or give advice to individuals who are in disadvantaged or vulnerable positions such as abusive relationships, oppression, poverty, mental illness, disability, or such positions that may be considered underprivileged. Such individuals would need the gospel for the underprivileged. Since most of us are privileged in some areas in our lives and possibly underprivileged in other areas, it is important to keep in mind how this book may apply differently to unique aspects of our lives.

My Approach

As I am a "Privileged Western White American Christian," I write as one who has been examining my own Christian tradition. I am attempting to understand where my perceptions might be skewed and how my perceptions can be brought more in line with how Christ sees the world. I have struggled with my privilege because it seems that many parts of the Bible make it clear that the words "privileged Christian" are oxymoronic (to be touched on later). This book is an attempt to understand my place in Christianity and the church whilst living in a privileged society. The basic assumption that I write from is that *the highest understanding of life and its meaning comes from looking at God.* Coincidentally, I have found much insight and understanding by considering the general theme of "the image of God" in relation to the present situation. I have concluded, quite unoriginally, that we are called to be like Christ and reveal God's image to the world; therefore, the primary question this book attempts to address is: *what does it mean to be a Christian and reveal God's image while living in a privileged society?*

Subject

This book is the result of my wrestling with that question. Perhaps, by exploring the image of God and what it means to live a Christian life from a privileged position we can get away from some of the language that we are so used to in order to help us to see the Christian life through fresh eyes. As I answer this question, I provide a "new vision" for how Christianity can look in the Privileged World (It is not a new vision at all, for it is as old as Christ).

In Chapter 1, I begin with a quick overview explaining why I think the gospel needs to be reframed for the privileged and how this new perspective of the gospel will lead us forward. I then examine the "big picture" in Chapter 2 by looking at the Biblical story and its culmination in the crucified Christ as it relates to our calling in life. Chapter 3 seeks to examine the meat of our callings as Christians through an emphasis on imitating Christ in both humility and authority. Chapters 4 and 5 emphasize the universal scope of our calling and attempts to explore how we can see the world through Christ's eyes. Chapter 6 and 7 discuss the gift and calling of diversity of the privileged church as well as the challenges associated with such a vision. Chapter 8 concludes the book with a reflection on the glorious, life-giving, and abundant life God is calling us privileged Christians to partake in.

Great read map.

Well written...

Throughout this book, I provide many criticisms of privileged Christianity. Often, my discussion of privileged Christianity might come off as "harsh" or borderline "too challenging" to some readers. Harsh and challenging ideas will inevitably cause us to feel defensive and outrightly reject such ideas; however, I believe that if we humbly and thoughtfully consider the implications of challenging ideas (even if we may not ever fully agree with such), we tend to grow in our ability to see the world as God intends. Further, I wish to emphasize that I do not intend to offend, but to challenge. So, when I criticize aspects of privileged Christianity, understand that I, the writer, am as much challenged in my thinking and lifestyle as you, the reader. In a way, this book is a letter to myself pointing out many ways that I need to be challenged and areas in which I need to grow. Perhaps, this is why I use such a harsh tone at times – it's to wake myself up as much as it might wake the reader up. So please do not be too offended - I am just as offended.

In the end, the Christian life is one of becoming like Christ – as an individual and as a church – both, of which, are to be intertwined and inseparable. This book has largely focused on my reflections on what it means to be privileged and to live like Christ. I would like to emphasize that we do not become Christlike purely through obedience to his commands or the law, but we become Christlike through God transforming our hearts and personhoods into the type of person that naturally obeys the law of Christ. Without this transformation of the heart, our efforts to obey (no matter how radical) will be birthed out of a false righteousness and ultimately fail. Truly, nothing could be more important than becoming like Christ. To summarize: in humility, in authority, in community, in our oneness, in truth, in love, we are supposed to be like Christ. Yet, mere words cannot summarize Christ, for he is a person; and, the person of Christ transcends language. Therefore, where we really learn to be like Christ is not through a book, but through our experiences with him and his community (the church). That is why I emphasize the importance of community, diversity, suffering, service, and prayer and action as the means by which we are transformed into his image. And, when we are transformed into his image, the world and us catch a glimpse of Jesus. And, it is in these glimpses that the world will come to see Christ as the one whose name is above every name and who deserves all the glory. But, that is all easier said than done… I better stop before I give away too much.

And before you continue, I ask that you join me in a simple prayer before continuing to read:

Jesus, help us.
Thank you,
Amen.

1

THE GOSPEL FOR THE PRIVILEGED

Shout! A full-throated shout! Hold nothing back—a trumpet-blast shout! Tell my people what's wrong with their lives... They're busy, busy, busy at worship, and love studying all about me. To all appearances they're a nation of right-living people— law-abiding, God-honoring.

They ask me, "What's the right thing to do?" and love having me on their side. But they also complain, "Why do we fast and you don't look our way? Why do we humble ourselves and you don't even notice?"

Isaiah 58:1-3 MSG

The Irrelevant Gospel

Recognizing our Privilege

I am not a theologian as I have no formal training in the study of scripture. Yet, I do not think it takes a "theologian" to understand all that Jesus challenges the church to. As I've pursued Jesus, I have been convicted and convinced that the way Christianity is practiced in privileged contexts is far from the original vision and heart of Christ. This is the root of my spiritual dissonance. I propose that the reason we have gotten so far from the message of Christ is because a gospel is being preached that is *irrelevant* to the privileged church. Before you say, *"Wait, what? How dare he call the gospel irrelevant,"* please hear me out.

First off, it seems that today, many sections of the Bible are left out of our worship songs, our Christian discussions, and many of our sermons. The neglect, willful ignorance, or plain misinterpretation of certain teachings of Jesus has come to a point where the message is irrelevant to the life of the privileged church. The gospel is reduced to nothing more than a motivational talk on "being a better person" or "being happy, healthy, and wise." It is irrelevant because it usually does not radically change the way we live. And, if it ever does "radically" change people, it is usually in a legalistic and/or conspiratorial* way that is completely counter to the gospel itself. Most commonly, legalistic and conspiratorial thinking mixes with a sort of materialism that produces an irrelevant and harmful gospel.

Or maybe it is not that it is irrelevant, but that it seems to have been taken out of context and misconstrued (albeit, often unintentionally and subconsciously) to excuse the hierarchical structures of the world which allow a privileged few to live a life of luxury while most of the world lives off virtually nothing. *Wow,* that escalated quickly, and I hope that my proposal is not lost in the last sentence. And I hope it is clear when I say the "privileged few," I do not mean the billionaires and millionaires; I am talking about just about every person who lives in the Privileged World. *We are the privileged few,* for even our poor have more

---

* *Conspiratorial,* meaning a sense that "the world is out to get them" and that they must do something to prevent this. Related to this are the certain concocted theological themes that are emphasized – especially pertaining to the "apocalypse" or "second coming:" prophecies, rapture, Israeli statehood, and political expediency.

money, opportunity, and health than what the average person around the world will ever have in life.*

Here's a couple quick stats just to give you a snapshot: if your income is $30,000 USD per year you make more than 98.8% of people in the world and 58% of people in the world make less than $1000 USD every year.[1] Not even to mention the privilege we have in healthcare access, educational opportunities, safety, freedom, etcetera. The reality is that we live in an impoverished world – of which, we are at the top. It is objectively quite strange that we are so rich, yet we often don't recognize that we are so privileged. We take such privilege as a normal part of life when it is actually an exception to the normal human experience. If we fail to acknowledge our privilege and seriously consider how this uniquely impacts our call as Christians – the gospel will remain irrelevant and misunderstood in our society.

Let's go back to a claim I made on the last page: that the gospel excuses *"the hierarchical structures of the world which allow a privileged few to live a life of luxury while most of the world lives off of virtually nothing."* In what ways has the gospel been misconstrued to excuse this? I do not wish to go in depth on this point, but I wish to make it clear that almost no Christian would outrightly admit that this is something the gospel teaches. However, I believe that the culture of privilege has seeped into the church in a way that has created a subtext that excuses this unconscious viewpoint. After all, *we have earned our privilege through hard*

---

* To be clear, the idea that the poor among us have more than many of the poor around the world should not be used as an excuse to neglect the poor among us! Suffering in all forms and in all places should be our concern – whether that suffering occurs close to us or across the sea.

work, we live in the greatest country on earth, we deserve our privilege because of our Christian history and God's blessing... or so we've often been told. I dare say that this is none other than a false gospel brought about by partial preaching of the gospel. What if our privilege was a stumbling block that disadvantages us from being able to understand the gospel? What if, instead of a blessing, our privilege was a sort of "curse" that makes it more difficult for us to live a blessed abundant life?

A Disadvantaged Audience

To summarize, here is my reasoning (on a most simplistic level) for why the Bible, as we read and teach it, may be irrelevant for the privileged church today:

The epistles are written to churches while they were facing persecution and, in some cases, death for their allegiance to Christ. However, our church is not facing persecution; therefore, much of the apostolic exhortations and advice are not understood properly or are even applicable, for that matter.

Jesus' sermons are often addressed to a crowd of outcasts, poor, needy, sick, and humble-minded individuals. However, the privileged church is mostly full of middle-class White people – not usually the outcast, poor, needy, sick, and humble minded people.

Much of the psalmist's prayers are prayed by "the poor and needy"[2] asking God why the wicked prosper while they suffer. However, our church is full of prosperous individuals that if we were to pray the prayers of the Psalms, they would not be able to pray in the heart of the psalmist. How can we pray, *why do the wicked prosper?* While we, ourselves, are prospering?

Truly, the privileged church today is, by all means, not full of the persecuted, poor, needy, sick, humble-minded people (not to say that there aren't some corners of the church with such of *those people* tucked away). ~~More often than not, it is filled with upper-middle class individuals who are usually not outcasts of society.~~ It is filled with privileged people. As a result, much of scripture loses its relevance because it is lost in context.

A gospel framed for the poor is preached to the rich and well-off individuals of society. When we hear sermons about God's comfort, we apply them to situations such as when we didn't get promoted, when our sports team loses, when we feel stressed about having too many things to take care of, when we lose money on a bad investment, or even in the tragic loss of a loved one. Truly, in such situations we can and should go to God for comfort and a better perception, but the fullness of this message may be missed when this message of comfort was first preached to people who lost their livelihood, were oppressed by governing authorities, risked their lives, had friends die for their faith, and had terrorists stoning them in the streets. ~~Maybe we have yet to understand the fullness of God's provision of comfort and peace partly because we haven't ever experienced or embraced the full, equally good, "uncomfortable," life Jesus calls us to.~~

When we come across the challenging and radical sayings of Jesus, our minds are so mired with the culture of privilege (partly due to the glib statements of many pastors that make light these radical challenges) that we are completely unable to receive Jesus' message with the same purity, innocence, or shock that the first disciples experienced. I was recently at a wedding where the pastor talked about Christlike sacrificial love and, in jovial seriousness, equated it to sacrificing one's hair appointment so her husband can afford a night out with some friends. But in reality, this message of sacrifice was meant for those who had to risk everything (safety, career, life, and maybe even family) to become a Christian. We hear a message on not worrying and we apply it to whether we will be able to send our child to a great university or whether we will pay our mortgage on our houses. All the while, this message of not worrying was meant for those who didn't know where their next meal was coming from, if they could afford clothing, or find a place to stay the night. The same goes for the messages on trust, patience (longsuffering), love, grace, humility, etc. Much of the Bible as it was written is "lost in translation" – that is contextual and cultural translation.

Worse still, the gospel meant for the poor and needy is preached to the privileged and secure, and as a result, the privileged end up deceiving themselves into thinking they are poor, needy, persecuted, and faced with worrisome events each day. No wonder there seems to be much insecurity and anxiety even though such prosperity has never been seen before in history. The result is a Christianity that is seen as weak and laughable in the eyes of the global church. Christianity has become so comfortably wrapped up in a privileged society that the gospel has lost its immediate relevance. No longer do we need the *daily bread* to survive, we can simply use our bank card at the grocery store for that. We need not God as our *refuge and strength* for we have that in our armies. We no longer need Jesus, the great physician, for we have access to the best doctors available. Instead, the daily bread, refuge and strength, and healing powers of Jesus are quaint ideas that we add to our pile of "blessings" but rarely ever put our weight on. Such promises of Jesus are not as relevant to us since most of us are not going hungry, lacking shelter, and suffering from untreated illnesses.

To be clear, I am not necessarily saying that we are supposed to pursue such hardships; yet, I am saying that because of privilege (and lack of hardship), our gospel perspective is faulty and needs to change if we are to understand it better.

A Poor Man's Religion

The good news of Jesus was meant for the poor. Jesus himself proclaims, "The Spirit of the Lord is on me, because he has anointed me to proclaim good news *to the poor*. He has sent me to proclaim freedom for the prisoners, and recovery of sight for *the blind*, to set *the oppressed* free, to proclaim the year of the Lord's favor."[3] If this is what Jesus proclaimed, we should find that those who hold most tightly to Jesus' message are the poor, the disabled, and those without basic rights – the definitively underprivileged of this world. In truth, in much of the world, Christianity could be considered the "religion of the poor." India, for example, provides a pointed example in which 50-90% of the Christians there come from the poorest of the poor, the so-called "untouchable" class.*[4] All the while, there is much resistance toward Christ among higher caste individuals

---

* A relic of traditional Hinduism is what is known as "the caste system." In this system individuals are grouped into four "castes" based on the family that they are born into. One is not supposed to marry outside of their caste and is not allowed to pursue professions outside of their class. Untouchables are those who don't have a caste and are only allowed to pick through the garbage for a living. Although this system's visibility is slowly fading away in India, its existence may reveal something about the nature of humanity.

because becoming a Christian would require them to leave the place of social privilege that they possess in Hinduism's caste system. Either that, or the high-class become Christians and only associate with other high-class Christians while continuing to oppress the lower classes. Such a "Christian" has not yet understood the gospel.

It is safe to assume that most well-off, healthy, and free individuals don't feel the deep need for a benefactor, a healer, nor a freedom fighter (which is certainly why many privileged individuals reject him). If well-off individuals were to accept Jesus, it would mean that they should join in Jesus' freedom fighting vocation. And, if we should learn from history, freedom is not obtained without much sacrifice – whether that be physical freedom, political freedom, or spiritual freedom. There is much incentive for the well-off to reject or distort Jesus; for, if we were to embrace Jesus' kingdom as our reality – it would inevitably mean the privileged would have to lay down some of their privilege for the sake of the underprivileged (more on that later).

The present situation the West lives in – one in which most Christians *are* well-off – is a unique rarity that almost seems ironic in light of the message of Jesus. This seems to testify to two things. First, it testifies that "nothing is impossible with God" for even the rich can be saved.[5] Secondly, it testifies that perhaps we have compromised parts of Jesus' message; particularly, it seems that we have removed *the requirement* to give up one's privilege when one comes to Christ.* Partly, this is missed as a requirement of

---

* Yes, I say "requirement." If you are not yet convinced that this is a requirement of a Christian – keep reading and seek to understand what I am saying (even if you may not agree). Wrestle for yourself: "might this really be a requirement of the Christian call?"

the faith because there are not oppressive authorities or cultural norms strictly enforcing these requirements (as there are in many places where Christians are persecuted). Since laying down our privilege is "voluntary" in our culture, it is something one rarely does. Yet, it should not matter whether the culture strips us of our privilege when we follow Jesus or if we voluntarily lay it down. Jesus himself attests to the voluntary nature of laying down one's life and privilege: *No one takes my life from me, but I lay it down voluntarily – of my own accord.*[6] If we are to follow in Christ's footsteps, we too are called to voluntarily lay down our privilege and even our lives – regardless of our context. Coming to Christ in a privileged context should be no less radical than coming to Christ in a persecuted context. The cost of discipleship is to be no more costly in a persecuted context than it is in a privileged context – both, have the same call of Christ.

However, since we have seemingly removed this requirement from privileged Christians, perhaps we should wrestle an idea: We may not be all that different from the high caste Hindu who becomes a Christian and still abides by the caste system and enjoys the fruits of it; all the while, ignoring the millions of untouchable-least-of-these that are brutally discriminated against. It may be hard to identify such a spirit within ourselves because we do not explicitly come face to face with such disparities because our culture does not practice such an explicit caste system (we, at least, might have this a partial excuse for our blindness[*]).

---

[*] In the first place, we only have this excuse for blindness because we have become privileged enough that we have been able to hide away those in our own society that are poor and hungry. In our suburbs, we have insulated ourselves from the vast injustices and poverty that exists even within our own cities.

Nevertheless, it seems that there might be an "invisible global caste system" in which those at the top feel they have the right to a certain standard of living simply because of their place of birth. Christians living at the top of this global caste system should seriously consider what it means to receive a message of freedom, healing, and good news that Jesus proclaimed was for the poor and needy.

A Whole Gospel

Certainly, this gospel is the gospel for the human condition*; it is absolutely beautiful and should be preached and understood by all – even the privileged. The messages of freedom, healing, and good news are essential for all to hear – regardless of their context. Every meaningful Christian walk must begin with the realization that, without Christ, one is utterly enslaved to sin, utterly sick of heart, and utterly without hope. The messages of freedom, healing, and good news are the essential starting points of the Christian walk for all. And we must return over-and-over to these messages throughout our lives.

For those who are physically oppressed, physically disabled, and physically hopeless – these messages will be all the more applicable and important to focus on. But, for those who are privileged enough to be unoppressed, physically healthy, and provided for - Jesus has a message that goes *beyond* freedom, health, and hope.

It seems quite silly for privileged Christians to focus primarily on these messages of freedom, healing, and good news when Jesus had quite a *different* (or, I should say, *additional*) message for the privileged. It is akin to a healthy

---

* What is the "human condition" – we'll talk more about that in Chapter 2.

individual going to the doctor every week to hear themselves proclaimed healthy. Such a message becomes little more than a pat on the back. Perhaps, the privileged (healthy and free) should consider what they are called to do with their health and freedom lest the messages of health and freedom become insignificant and, even, irrelevant to their lives.

We must not stop at the "spiritual dimensions" (the inner life) of faith and neglect the "physical dimensions" (the outer life) of faith; if we do, our faith will be depressingly shallow and have no meaningful influence on our lives. Jesus does not let the privileged off so easily that all we must do is admit "spiritual poverty" and the Christian life is ours to keep. Jesus repeatedly exhorts the privileged (religiously, materially, or otherwise) to the effect of indicating that their eager grasp on privilege is the very evidence of their hypocrisy. One cannot claim to have "spiritual poverty" while, at the same time, refusing to identify with the physically poor and needy. And, one cannot truly identify with the physically poor and needy if they hold an eager grasp on their physically privileged position in life. To think one can be in solidarity with the poor while living in abundance is completely oxymoronic and evidences an internal disposition of spiritual superiority and privilege.

I am sure the pharisees and other religious elite enjoyed hearing Jesus' words of peace, comfort, and freedom (for, Israel was under foreign occupation at this time). Yet, as soon as Jesus started insisting that *they* wouldn't truly understand the real meaning of these messages until they shed themselves of their privileged positions, they utterly despised Jesus. Jesus' emphasis on self-surrender made his message incomprehensible for those who had too much to lose by such surrender. In the same way, might we hear the "good" messages of Jesus with enjoyment; but, as soon as Jesus' message takes aim at our privilege, we quietly back away or insist that Jesus meant something other than what he said.

We conveniently claim all the good news, comfort, blessedness, freedom, and sight that comes from identifying ourselves with the gospel for the poor and needy. But, Jesus' message insists that we cannot lump ourselves in with the poor when it is convenient for us and distance ourselves from them when such identification becomes inconvenient. One cannot be spiritually impoverished (in the way God desires) if one holds onto physical privilege without being willing to lay it down for the sake of the underprivileged. Until we take up the plight of the poor as our very own plight, we have not begun to live such a way that identifies with the poor and needy. And, until we identify with the poor we cannot truly receive the gospel for the poor and needy.

In truth, when Jesus first taught in the Synagogue, he read those words from Isaiah, (*good news to the poor, freedom for the prisoners and oppressed, and God's favor*) Luke says that "all spoke well of him and were amazed at the gracious words that came from his lips."[7] His audience was probably thinking of themselves as the poor and oppressed – after all, they were under foreign occupation. They were *amazed* at his gracious message. Yet, Jesus recognized that his audience was also privileged and had an attitude of superiority in many regards. Luke says he then got up and continued to recount story after story about God having grace on Israel's ethnic outsider "inferiors" and not on Israel itself. Jesus' audience had been ready to rejoice upon hearing his gracious words, but when Jesus began to take aim at his audience's attitudes of superiority and despise of the underprivileged, they responded by trying to push him off a cliff! Would it not be the same in the average privileged church if a pastor preached a message of grace and freedom, and then at the end of it started talking about the immigrant, racism, "systemic injustice" or "White privilege"? It is no wonder that our preachers today limit their messages to love, grace, hope, and other nice things without going beyond those messages. The privileged prefer a shallow *partial gospel* to a whole gospel that requires a deep shift in one's thinking and attitude.

[handwritten margin note: Probably kse because of "CRT"...]

Unless we deal with our privilege as Jesus would have us, we run the risk of being *admirers* of Jesus rather than his *disciples.* In one interaction with a privileged admirer, *Jesus lovingly looked at the rich young man and said, "One thing you still lack: Go, sell everything you have and give to the poor and you will have treasure in heaven. Then, come, follow me." At this, the man's face fell. He went away sad because he had great wealth.*[8]

Jesus asks much of those who have much. He asks much because their privilege has put them diametrically opposed to the kingdom. They are opposed to the kingdom because their hearts are corrupted by privilege. They are the most impoverished because they have the most difficulty seeing their own sad state. They are in a sad state because they cannot enter the kingdom of heaven as long as they are in this state. They cannot enter the kingdom because there is no room in the kingdom for those who treasure privilege over the things of the kingdom (such as justice, mercy, and humility). *For where your treasure is, there your heart will be also.*[9]

Again, Jesus asks much because privilege places people in diametrical opposition to the kingdom. No one ever receives or experiences Jesus in the context of their own power and worth. Rather, people receive Jesus in the context of understanding they have nothing – absolutely nothing – and that Jesus is everything.

The Relevant Gospel

We, like the pharisees and the rich young man, love the beautiful passages on God's cause for the poor ("The Gospel for the Poor and Needy"); meanwhile, much of the "gospel for the privileged" is neglected when it is the most relevant to our current situation! Here is the "good-news-gospel" Jesus preached for the privileged: *Woe to the rich, woe to the well-fed, woe to those who laugh now, woe to those who are spoken well of*[10]. *Woe - how sad is it for those who live in such states...* I guess that doesn't sound exactly like good news – in reality, it sounds more like a curse to be all of the above! We certainly have a large misunderstanding of what it is to be blessed! Anyone who is well-fed, happy-go-lucky, rich, or popular ought to feel uncomfortable when hearing those words of Jesus – I certainly do. Jesus' message to the privileged is one of challenge and uncomfortability; indeed, this is why we avoid preaching sermons or meditating on such *woes*.

In addition to many sayings of Jesus, many other scripture passages are aimed at the privileged (i.e., the prophets and John the Baptist). And, it is never the "comforting message" like the gospel for the poor and needy. Anytime Jesus encounters privileged people, there is often some sort of confrontation: The religiously privileged he calls a "brood of vipers,"[11] "children of the devil,"[12] and constantly offends them with his teaching. The materialistically privileged, he tells to "sell all he has and give to the poor."[13] Still, in some cases, he encounters the privileged (who are usually some sort of outcast in one manner or another), and they end up giving up all their privilege for the cause of righteous justice. Think of Zacchaeus the tax collector – hated by his own people yet rich from his alliance with the Romans – and how Jesus welcomed him despite the chagrin of the Pharisees. And in response, Zacchaeus proclaimed that he would give half his possessions to the poor and pay back fourfold anyone he had cheated.[14]

Jesus seemed to have had little patience for the privileged. He wanted to preach to the poor and needy – but he still made it clear what the privileged should do – *leverage and lay-down one's privilege for the sake of the underprivileged* (to be discussed in more detail later). Yet, one of the main concerns of privileged preachers today is often to attract individuals who can give out of their wealth to the ministry so that their church buildings can be "upgraded" to attract more privileged people. It is as if we renounce the global caste system in word, and then live by it in deed – and still expect to receive the blessedness that God extends to those who live on the bottom of this system (i.e., "blessed are the poor").

Perhaps the *most relevant* parts of the Bible for the privileged Church today would be *the prophets*. The prophets – aimed often at the social and religious elite – called out the privileged for their arrogant and ignorant lifestyles. "For day after day they seek me out; they seem eager to know my ways, as if they were a nation that does what is right and has not forsaken the commands of its God. They ask me for just decisions and seem eager for God to come near them,"[15] but God responds in saying, "Is not this the kind of fasting I have chosen: to loosen the chains of injustice and untie the cords of the yoke, to set the oppressed free and break every yoke? Is it not to share your food with the hungry and to provide the poor wanderer with shelter— when you see the naked, to clothe them, and not to turn away from your own flesh and blood?."[16] Surely, this is a relevant message for the privileged Church today – a message that was also strongly preached by the way Jesus himself lived his life. Yet, it doesn't seem that much emphasis is placed on these passages in the prophets. Instead, if we turn to the prophets, we are more likely to turn to the passages that were used to comfort and give hope to oppressed and exiled people groups! Perhaps because they are more palatable and enjoyable than the harsh rebuke of the prophet.

Phillip Jenkins emphasizes that "passages (in the Bible) that seem mildly embarrassing for a Western audience read completely differently, and relevantly, in the new churches of Africa or Latin America."[17] This is because other Christians around the world often fit the mold of what would be considered "poor and needy" and, in the last century, sometimes being a Christian meant much more risk was required of the individual than was expected in the West (i.e. involvement in the fight for liberation from oppressors, living amidst corrupt governments, real religious persecution, etc.). What's more, common reports of healings and miracles come out of such churches and have come to be expected as a normal part of the Christian walk. So, when we are sheepish or hesitant about Jesus' commands to heal physical disease, there is a whole other side of the world that is rejoicing because they see it as a normal part of the church. I do not wish to paint a picture that the churches in Africa and Latin America are "doing everything right," but I only wish to point out what things we, the privileged church, may be missing in our walk with God. Our privilege has, in many ways, hindered our walk with Christ and our ability to understand the Bible; yet, if we refuse to settle for a shallow understanding of the gospel, we will find ourselves discovering a whole new rich life in Christ.

Worse still, not only does our privilege hinder our walk, but our current position may put us at odds with Christ himself. Many Christians today seem to be mourning the loss of influence that the gospel has had on the increasingly resistant culture of our society. Saddened by the fading influence, popular culture and younger generations are often blamed. However, I would argue that the gospel has not lost its influence because of a changing culture; it has lost its influence because the culture of privilege has so compromised the church. This has resulted in a watered-down, lukewarm gospel that is easier for the privileged to stomach. But, Jesus makes it clear what he thinks of such a gospel. Jesus, in addressing a particularly well-off group of Christians, says,

> "I know your deeds, that you are neither cold nor hot. I wish you were either one or the other! So, because you are lukewarm—neither hot nor cold—I am about to spit you out of my mouth. You say, '*I am rich; I have acquired wealth and do not need a thing.*' But you do not realize that you are wretched, pitiful, poor, blind and naked."[18]

This should come as a staunch warning to the dangers of prosperity, contentment, comfort, and wealth. Our very position of privilege puts us at risk of Jesus spitting us out of his mouth. And, no doubt, the world will want to spit us out of their mouths as well. Thankfully, Jesus also gives direction to how the privileged can receive the gospel:

> "I counsel you to buy from me gold refined in the fire, so you can become rich; and white clothes to wear, so you can cover your shameful nakedness; and salve to put on your eyes, so you can see. Those whom I love I rebuke and discipline. So be earnest and repent. Here I am! I stand at the door and knock. If anyone hears my voice and opens the door, I will come in and eat with that person, and they with me."

From a kingdom perspective, the poor are the ones who are blessed, while the rich are the ones who are blind and dressed in rags. What we consider *worldly privileges* are actually *heavenly disadvantages*. This is utterly backwards to the way we usually think! Until we realize what a pitiful state we are in, we live a delusional life in which we are deaf and blind without knowing it. Therefore, let us seek to truly *hear his voice* that we may *open the door* and *share a meal* with Christ. And, if our sight is ever to be restored and if we are to escape this shameful state, we must buy the gold refined in the fire – treasure in heaven that comes through justice, mercy, and humility rather than spending our lives on temporary treasures that put us at odds with who Jesus wants us to become.

Good News for the Privileged

I must stop rattling on lest I steal from the latter parts of this book. In this chapter, we have considered that a "new gospel" needs to be preached to the privileged. Throughout this book, we will explore what this type of gospel might look like in more detail and perhaps rediscover the type of life Jesus is calling us to. From what I have written so far, it would seem that the "gospel" is more like "bad news" and condemnation for the privileged. And, it certainly is bad news from a worldly perspective, but from a kingdom perspective, it is great news. God has a specific place in his story for Christians in privileged contexts. There is a deep and meaningful call on our lives. It is only bad news for the privileged if we ignore the call of Jesus, but it is the best news when we enter the abundant life Jesus calls us to. I truly think that these are beautiful times and that this calling of the privileged church has the potential to bring revival and newness to Christianity in the West.

The gospel (aka "good news") is not just something that we receive and intellectually acknowledge as true; it is something that we receive into our very being and are transformed by. We then become living, breathing gospels following in the footsteps of Christ. For, *I have been crucified with Christ, and I no longer live, but Christ lives in me.*[19] In this sense, the "gospel for the privileged" is simply a summary of what Jesus would do if he were privileged. We must stop simply *receiving* the gospel and move on to *living* the gospel. *Receiving the gospel* is primarily about our own personal salvation, while *living the gospel* is ultimately about bringing salvation to others. If we stop at one or the other, we get an incomplete gospel that, dare I say, brings about incomplete salvation. The gospel for the privileged is good news because it is an invitation to enter into the *whole gospel* that leads to abundant life, as opposed to a mediocre life.

It is for this very reason that I am convinced that this gospel for the privileged is not bad news, but certainly is good news! What's more, the moment we accept Christ's message for the privileged and put it into practice, Christ's message for the poor and needy becomes relevant to us as well. Ultimately, the gospel has lost its relevance in the Western church because it is largely unpracticed in its basic form. We receive a warped gospel designed to suit our lifestyles. If we truly practice the gospel for the privileged and well-off, then, certainly, we will receive the gospel for the poor and needy in its fullness; for when we lay down our privilege, we may find ourselves in a position of being poor and needy. The gospel comes full circle; the gospel for the privileged and the gospel for the poor and needy are united into one.

Until we come to terms with the whole gospel, many aspects of the gospel will remain irrelevant for our lives. It is time we re-orient our Christian life and focus on the words that apply to Christians coming from privileged positions. Ultimately, this re-orientation begins by going back to the basics of our Christian faith and understanding how God reveals himself in the world. It also begins by looking at what the gospel means for the current context that we live in.

In its shortest form, this is the gospel I am convinced Jesus preaches to the privileged:

> *To lay down and leverage one's privilege for*
> *the sake of the underprivileged in the name*
> *and Spirit of Christ. And in doing so, we die*
> *to ourselves so the life of Christ may flow*

through us. This is good news because nothing
is better than the life that flows from Christ.

2

HUMANITY'S REDEMPTION SONG

Who believes what we've heard and seen? Who would have thought GOD's saving power would look like this?

Isaiah 53:1 MSG

Still, it's what GOD had in mind all along, to crush him with pain. The plan was that he give himself as an offering for sin so that he'd see life come from it—life, life, and more life. And GOD's plan will deeply prosper through him.

Isaiah 53:10 MSG

Before we can fully understand the kind of life God calls privileged people to, we ought to look at the kind of life God intends for *all* humans regardless of context. In essence, we ought to have a firm understanding of what it means to be human in light of what God has revealed to humanity.*

I propose that the basic understanding of what it means to be human is found in the idea that we are made in the image of God. It makes sense to start here because it is where God started with humanity. When God created humanity, he said, "Let us make human beings in our image,

---

* I could never provide that firm understanding of "the meaning of life" in a little chapter, but this chapter may at least provide a starting point.

to be like us."[1] So, at our core, we are made to be like God, to reflect his image.

But what does it really mean that to be made in the "image of God"? It is kind of a difficult concept to understand at face value. I mean, I have heard many quaint (and probably true) things about this: *We have more complex minds than the animals; therefore, that must be a reflection of who God is; among all creation, we are the only ones made in the image of God; therefore, humans must be special among creation; God is the ruler of everything, we reflect his image by being the rulers of the earth.*

All of these must be true to a certain extent, but I have always been left wanting for a deeper understanding of what this really means. I think the essence of what it means to be made in God's image is simply that *God intends us to be like him and share in his abundant life and abundant love.* Since we are made in God's image, we are well on track to try to understand what God is like. For, by looking at God and getting to know him, we are also getting a good look at what God intends for his created humanity. Knowing God, therefore, becomes the most meaningful means by which we can understand the nature and purpose of humanity.

As Christians, we base much of our knowledge of God on what is written about him in the Bible. It is generally accepted that God progressively reveals himself throughout scripture. This means that God's character, nature, and essence are built upon throughout scripture, culminating in Jesus Christ as the ultimate and most perfect revelation of who God is. Therefore, as we journey through scripture, we catch glimpses of the God that humans were modelled after and were created to be like – while the ultimate understanding of God's intention for humanity is found in the person of Jesus.

The Garden

Starting in the Garden of Eden, we see the first glimpses of what humanity's relationship with God was like. Upon reading Genesis 3:8, A.W. Tozer[2] emphasizes that "God and man walked together and because the Creator had made man in his own image there was no degradation in His communion with man." Humans walked on the same plane as God – with him, and in his image – created to relate to him as one relates to their own kind. Humanity is created in *original blessing* and divine connectedness. "God saw what he had made, and it was *very good.*"[3]

This communion that man and God shared was broken when man rejected God. Ironically, the serpent said humanity would be "like God" if he ate the fruit, but in doing so, he became "fallen man" and, consequently, became a fallen image of God.[4] In a twisted turn of events, humans were convinced they needed to become something they already inherently were ("like God") and were deceived into thinking God was trying to keep them from having abundant life. Such thinking and behavior blinded humans from being able to see God as he is and as a result, we became disconnected from our true selves. ~~The intimate communion with God which allowed humans to reflect his image was broken, and humanity lost its ability to live the abundant life God intended.~~

At "the fall," humanity lost the ability to fully reflect God's image and lost the ability to clearly see God's image as it is; therefore, humanity became ever confused at how to regain God's image. It seems as if since then, humanity has been confused as to what humanity is supposed to be and has ever been trying to regain the fullness of the "divine spark" that once enabled us to live life to the fullest. A lost image of God has led to a loss of purpose. Nevertheless, humanity still retained the image of God, for it was built into their nature, as the image of God is still built into our nature today; the fall could not change this fundamental part of our humanity, but it caused things to become a little less clear – like peering through a dirty window. Today, we find ourselves peering through that same dirty window.

Humanity, no longer in perfect relationship with God, no longer has direct access to what humanity was modelled after. Therefore, the purpose of life became confused.

Progressive Revelation

Throughout Scripture, it seems that God is trying to show his people what he is like. Repeatedly, God speaks, "Here I am, this is what I am like, and I want to be in relationship with you." Through Abraham, through Moses, through David, and through the Prophets, God revealed himself more and more. Yet, it seems that fallen humanity has a propensity for a warped view of God and completely misunderstanding his message.

Often, his people thought they could restore relationship with God if they created laws, meticulously obeyed them, did violence in God's name, and sacrificed animals to appease God. It gets to the point where God explicitly tells his people, "I desire mercy, not sacrifice,"[5] "to obey is better than sacrifice"[6] (i.e., obedience doesn't mean religious duty), "righteousness and justice are more pleasing to God than sacrificial offerings,"[7] and even, "What makes you think I want all your sacrifices? I am sick of your burnt offerings of rams and the fat of fattened cattle. I get no pleasure from the blood of bulls and lambs and goats."[8] Instead, "He has told you, O man, what is good; and what does the Lord require of you but to do justice, and to love kindness, and to walk humbly with your God?"[9]

Yet, as clearly as God put it, his message rarely seems to get through to humanity. While God repeatedly seemed to say, "here I am, this is what I am like, this is the kind of life I have for you" repeatedly in the Old Testament, the people still didn't quite get it. Hence, he came and said, "HERE I AM, THIS IS WHAT I AM LIKE, THIS IS THE KIND OF LIFE I HAVE FOR YOU" when he himself came in human flesh as *the visible image of the invisible God;*[10] And, it still seems that many of us haven't gotten it yet. Even as he made his very home among us.

Up until Jesus' incarnation, God's people (Israel) seemed to have been convinced that humanity was completely unholy and unworthy to be close to God – the psalmist expresses this in saying, "surely I was sinful at birth, sinful from the time my mother conceived me"[11] and in frustration at the distance between God and man Job proclaimed, "He is not a man like me that we might confront each other in court… If only there was someone to mediate between us, someone to bring us together… Then I would speak out without fear of him, but as it now stands with me, I cannot."[12] To the people in the Old Testament, humanity was in a permanently degraded form, and to be human was the same as to be corrupted – completely unable to commune with a holy God. One might say they imagined humanity to be steeped in "original sin," as many still do today. *[Is this a denial of original sin? — handwritten marginal note]*

Yet, if by simply being human, one was evil, Jesus becoming human would have corrupted him. By no means was God corrupted in this. In fact, when Christ became man, he did not degrade the godhead. The glory of humanity is lifted to a status that it hadn't "achieved" since creation and

unless he was born of a virgin… — handwritten marginal note is being lifted, perhaps, to an even greater glory than that which was in the garden. God declared humanity good in the garden and reclaimed it as good by becoming human himself. Jesus proclaimed, once again, *original blessing* over humanity. Blessed humanity walks on the same plane as God in unbroken communion. Thus, the frustration of Job is addressed by God becoming man and mediator. Truly, Jesus is Emmanuel, *God with us.*

Jesus came to show us what God is like and, in effect, show us what God created humanity to be like. He came to reclaim humanity as his good creation made to be in relationship with him. Once again, man walks with God as he did in the garden and God breathes onto us his abundant life.

Jesus came to save from sin.
Mt 1:18-25

Incarnation

I feel like we often like to emphasize Jesus as being God, while Jesus liked to emphasize that he himself was a man. It is kind of funny. In *Luke,* Adam is listed as "Adam, the son of God"[13] while throughout the gospels, Jesus primarily refers to himself as "the Son of Man." I do not think that Luke nor Jesus did this unintentionally. Luke may have been highlighting that the origin of man was from God, and Jesus was highlighting that he (God) had become a man just like them.* Since the beginning of time, God intended a mysteriously intertwined connection between humanity and himself.

Along this line of thought, Paul considers Jesus the "second Adam."[14] Adam, in a way, represented humanity in

---

* In addition to possibly making reference to the Son of Man figure in Daniel 7.

that he was the father of all humanity; therefore, when Adam sinned it also meant that all of humanity sinned. But, as Adam represented humanity by being the father of all, Jesus represented humanity in that he was the son of all humanity. In Adam's case, he brought death through becoming a fallen image of God. In Jesus, life returned when humanity again had a perfect image of God. Adam lost the ability to live the abundant life that God intended, but Christ came that men "may have life, and have it to the full."[15]

By placing himself in the same storyline and history of Adam, Jesus identifies with mankind as a whole. This is reflected in that the name "Son of Man" could literally be translated as *"The Human."* A.W. Tozer[16] emphasizes that he was not just the Son of the Jews, but the Son of Humanity. N.T Wright[17] expands on this through an analysis of the Old Testament and indicates that Jesus represented Israel and therefore represented the whole of humanity. In the Old Testament[18] the Israelites were created to be a "kingdom of priests" that represents the whole of humanity to God; thus, when Jesus is representing Israel, he is representing all of humanity (including the privileged). He was the Son of all races, of all men; the incarnate body of the whole human race - *The Human*. He was the sum of all men wrapped up into one - not just symbolically, but in a mysterious sense.

Jesus was the *vicarious* representation of humanity to God. In summary, throughout Judaic history the high priest would *vicariously* represent the people to God on the Day of Atonement. This wasn't merely symbolical, for God would view the priest as the embodiment of Israel; thus, the sacrifice on the Day of Atonement would not just cover the sin of the priest but would cover the whole of Israel's sins.

In the same way, as the book of *Hebrews* discusses in depth, Jesus becomes the high priest embodying humanity to God. When God looks at Jesus (the vicarious embodiment of humanity), he sees not only Jesus, but also all of humanity.

Jesus' being human is a beautiful thing for humanity. God became approachable once again through him. In the Christian world, we often emphasize Jesus as God; thus, Jesus becomes more difficult for us to approach. In the non-believing world, it is emphasized that Jesus was merely a good man; thus, Jesus remains largely misunderstood and is perhaps *too easily* approached. We must emphasize, not just in words but with deep understanding that Jesus is both fully God and fully Man. This makes God approachable and glorifies humanity to a place of deep respect. Indeed, Jesus redeems man's image to its created glory and bestows upon man the glory of God (though this is not to be confused with making man equal to God). *Humanity is highly esteemed and sacred in the eyes of God; therefore, we should think of our fellow humans in the same way.*

Crucifixion

This series of events reaches its climax when the perfect image of God (Jesus) is sacrificed for the fallen image of God (the rest of humanity) so that fallen man may be redeemed and enter into the life man was created for. In essence, humanity wasn't properly reflecting what they were supposed to reflect, and as a result, the creator needed to reject and destroy this perversion of humanity in order to remake them into his image. But just any man wouldn't do, for any man wouldn't represent humanity as a whole; it needed to be someone who could embody humanity in a way that no one else could. Every man needed to be on the cross in order for God's plan to come to fullness. But, how did Jesus embody humanity in a way that no one else could? As already stated, Jesus called himself the Son of Man, or the Son of Humanity; thus, claiming to represent all of humanity. But what right did Jesus have to make this claim? Let me make the case, although, perhaps, imperfectly.

God created every individual human being in the image of God, and every individual is unique. Therefore, there are over seven billion unique expressions of the image of God. Albeit, seven billion fallen images of God. With so many unique images of the same God, this singular God must be infinitely massive and encompassing. What's more, if every person could be added together, it wouldn't come close revealing the complete massiveness of God. God's massiveness takes into account the uniqueness of every individual in earth. Therefore, only one who is in the perfect image of God can encompass humanity enough to represent all of humanity in one individual. And, since no human is the perfect image of God, only God can truly embody humanity. Therefore, Jesus, being both man and God, was the perfect image of God; and, thus, the perfect image of man. When Jesus walked the earth, he walked it in a way that he carried with him the image of every individual who has ever walked the earth. He represents every individual's God-bearing nature.

Jesus, is therefore, the good of every man wrapped up into one man. Yet, Jesus not only represents every individual's God-bearing nature but also represents every individual's sin-bearing nature. For, *He personally carried our sins in his body on the cross*[19] and *God made him who had no sin to be sin for us.*[20] Therefore, Jesus represented the whole human – righteous and sinful – when he hung on the cross.

On the cross, Jesus is the good of every man bearing the evil of every man. This reveals the very character of God as one who is willing to go to great lengths to bear our sin and bring us into relationship with him. Gregory Boyd says of such, "The offense of the cross is rather the declaration that the Word who united himself with our humanity in the incarnation went even further to unite himself with our sin and even with the God-forsaken curse that reflects all the self-destructive consequence of that sin!" The audacity of a perfect God who identifies with us while we are still sinners is why the cross may be seen as foolishness by some, but to sinners who identify with Jesus it is the very power of God![21]

Jesus represented all of humanity on the cross – all the beauty and brokenness of humanity collided in a single moment. In doing so, Jesus showed us what a God-bearing life looks like in a broken world – it is a life that bears and redeems brokenness. Paul exhorts that this is the way we, too, are to live: *Bear one another's burdens, and in this way, you fulfill the law of Christ.*[22] As beautiful as this is, it is also a little painful to come to grips with. I mean, we would like to think that God intends us to live a perfect life that is free from pain and burdens. Yet, on the cross, *Jesus shows us that a God-bearing life in a broken world is a life that bears other's sin and ugliness in a way that leads unto redemption.*

Resurrection

If the story ended with the crucifixion, we, as Christians, *are to be pitied most among all men;*[23] For death without resurrection is simply death as it was before Christ – sin and ugliness coming to irreversible completion. But, in resurrecting, Jesus' God-like bearing of sin gives way to

God-like redemption. Crucifixion is the bearing of sin and ugliness, and resurrection is the reversal of this sin and ugliness into beauty and glory. Jesus' goodness is able to take all of the evil into himself and come back bursting with life. Jesus was found worthy of bearing God's image and this worthiness has been transferred to all who follow Christ.

When reading the gospels, it is evident that the resurrected Christ was different from any other human that humanity had ever seen before. He is the "firstfruit of the dead"[24] – the firstborn of the new creation. This resurrected Christ wasn't an ordinary man like Lazarus, who rose from the dead. I imagine the very particles making up his body were dancing with new creation.

C.S. Lewis speaks of our present life as a life lived in the "shadowlands."[25] Shadowlands meaning that the new creation in heaven will make this earth seem like a fading dream that we had just woken up from and are soon forgetting. It is as if the new creation, the anticipated kingdom of heaven is so *Real* that it makes the reality of this world feel less real. Lewis says, "Heaven is reality itself. All that is fully real is Heavenly. For all that can be shaken will be shaken and only the unshakeable remains."[26] The hills - hillier than they ever were on earth, the air - more life-giving, and the mountains - more mountainous – dancing with the touch of God without an aspect of death and dying.

"For now we see things imperfectly, like puzzling reflections in a mirror, but then we will see everything with perfect clarity."[27] I imagine that this "perfect clarity" was what Jesus' resurrected body was like. Jesus' resurrection was physical, yet it transcended physicality as we know it. It was not *merely* a spiritual resurrection, but a perfect union between the divine breath and the physical flesh. It was as if every molecule in His body finally bore the essence of what creation was created to be and in doing so, His body became *more* physical and *more* real - so much more so that it goes beyond our real understanding. A physical body not bound by our constructs of physicality. He was unrecognizable by some until he made himself known, and he disappeared before some's very eyes.[28] Jesus passed through walls and appeared to the disciples.[29] The resurrected body now danced with the matter of heaven and it no longer was bound by the limits of earthly understanding. He is a stainless mirror reflecting the reality of God - The prototype of the new creation;[30] The firstfruit of a new humanity.

And if Jesus was the "first fruit," then there must be more fruit soon to ripen. When we are resurrected with Christ, we too will join Jesus in being stainless mirrors reflecting the reality of God. We too will be given new bodies that do not know the limitations our current bodies are bound to. Jesus' resurrection has profound implications for us, now and in the future. Paul explains the resulting reality that every Christian has experienced since the very beginning of the faith. Even now, as we live in our broken estate awaiting full redemption, *our present sufferings aren't even comparable to the glory that will be revealed in us. All creation waits in eager expectation for the children of God to be fully revealed* – for the new humanity to come into being. Since the fall of mankind, *creation has been suffering and frustrated,* incapable of the abundant life God desires because of man's conscious choice to reject him. Yet, *such futility has given way for hope. Creation will one day be liberated from slavery and brought into the glory and freedom possessed by the children of God.*

Even now, we are experiencing the firstfruit of the Spirit. This taste only whets our appetites for *adoption into sonship and the redemption of our bodies that comes when we experience the same resurrection as Jesus – bodies dancing with the touch of God and considered to be one of his own. This is our very hope that we wait for patiently and eagerly. All things are working toward this end. This has been his plan all along.* In fact, *God has set apart people, whom he has known since creation, to be conformed to the image of his Son. Jesus (the Son) is the firstborn of many brothers and sisters that embody the new humanity. And those he set apart, he also called; those he called, he also justified; those he justified, he also glorified.*[31] This is the trajectory that history and mankind was put on when the resurrection happened. What a privilege it is to live in a time where such mysteries have been revealed.

Ascension and Pentecost

After the resurrection, Jesus ascended to heaven to take his seat at the right hand of God. Today, the vision of Daniel has now come into reality and a Son of Man is sitting on the throne.[32] Sometimes, we think of the future reign of Christ and long for this future day. But the very fact that Jesus is sitting on the throne means that he is reigning today. Stephen, while being martyred proclaimed, "Look, I see heaven open and the Son of Man standing at the right hand of God."[33] This right-hand position means that his reign has begun, it is not something that is in the far-off future. The belief that Jesus is reigning *now*, *today*, should give the Christian much comfort, hope, and confidence for the present-day – not just platitudinal hope for the future; Jesus did not just leave us to our devices until he would one day come back. No, he reigns *now*, and his kingdom has arrived.

Soon after the ascension, the Holy Spirit arrived and animated the body of Christ in a way that produced an explosion of God's kingdom – an event that we are testimony of today. It is through his Holy Spirit that empowered people of God rule the earth as the body of Christ. Christ is the head; we are the body - God's new creation rule has begun. How magnificent. Still, we have yet to see the fullness of the kingdom. Therefore, we rejoice as we have seen the kingdom arrive, and anticipate as the kingdom is arriving in fullness. All one has to do is read *Acts* and the letters of Paul, to understand that the early church had a deep anticipation of this kingdom, a deep excitement. Sadly, we seem to have lost much of this excitement and anticipation.

I wish to emphasize here the important role the Holy Spirit plays in the life of the Christian church. In fact, the Holy Spirit is the very life of the Christian church. I feel like we often misunderstand the "Spirit of God" because we misunderstand what the word means, and we can't quite grasp what the "spirit" is because we don't have the mental categories for this. We are drawn to images of mysterious ghosts or the such, and when someone says they are "spiritual," we honestly have no idea what that means.

One thing that helped me better understand and envision what the Holy Spirit is, is learning the original meaning of the word. The Greek (*pneuma*) and Hebrew (*ruach*) words for Spirit mean "breath," "wind," or "air." Even the English word, spirit finds its origin in the Latin "Spiritus" which means *breath*. We are to think of the Holy Spirit as our very breath; something that the body of Christ cannot live without! We must be constantly breathing in (inspiring) the holy breath of God and breathing out (expiring) the breath of God out into the world. It is God's breath in our lungs – in our souls (sounds like a familiar worship song[34]). Not one human can survive one second without the sustaining work of the Spirit.

Yet, we misunderstand the Holy Spirit beyond just the meaning of the word. Often, we are left in disappointment, confusion, or fear when we talk about the Holy Spirit. We think it would've been better if Jesus would have just stayed. But Jesus said, "it is to your advantage that I go away, for if I do not go away, the Helper will not come to you. But if I go, I will send him to you."[35] This is a passage I think about often. Honestly, I so often wish that Jesus was still here and that I could see him in person. But, if we really trust Jesus, it is for our good that he has "left" because he has sent us his Spirit – the Helper. We must accept this as truth; the Spirit is exactly what we need in order to be transformed into the new kind of humanity God intends.

A.W. Tozer says that he is convinced that everything Jesus did on earth was done through the power of the Holy Spirit.[36] We like to think that Jesus was able to do everything he did and perform miracles because he was God – that all his healings were proof of divinity. But I think Tozer is correct in that everything Jesus did, it was through the empowering presence of the Holy Spirit in his life. When Jesus became man, he gave up the privileges of being God and "did not use it to his advantage." So, if Jesus did everything he accomplished through the power of the Holy Spirit, the same power that allowed Jesus' ministry such a miraculous accompaniment is the very same Spirit that lives within us. This is why Jesus said it would be to our advantage if he left - because he would send his Spirit to dwell within us. From Jesus' point of view, for everyone to have access to the same Spirit that was in him was much better for humanity as a whole. For, the physical body of Jesus can only be in one location on earth, but the Spirit can be everywhere. And now, the Spirit animates the body of Christ all over the world – making his presence and image known to people everywhere.

> Jesus said, "Peace be with you! As the Father sent me, I am sending you." And with that he *breathed* on them and said, "Receive the Holy Spirit." (John 20:21 NIV, Italics added)

The Body of Christ

With the advent of the Holy Spirit, human history entered the most exciting period up to that moment, and that period of history is continuing today. To emphasize again, Jesus himself said that *it is for your benefit that I am going away, for I am sending my Holy Spirit.*[37] It is the moment prophets had anticipated for generations and *yet did not see.*[38] It is the moment, where Peter proclaimed, that the prophets were being fulfilled and that the *Spirit was being poured out on all people.*[39] And, now, it is this present moment that creation has longed for and it is this present moment that signals the coming of a new kingdom that is not far off.

Yet, this Holy Spirit almost seems forgotten or neglected. I think this is partly due to God's preference to work through humanity to bring about his purposes and partly due to our lack of faith. Yet, I hold on to the truth of the Spirit being alive today. And it is this Spirit, the breath of God that still animates and gives life to His Body. It animates the body of Christ to being about God's purposes and it now animates our individual bodies to fulfill his purposes. Ultimately, the Spirit animates the Church and its individuals so that the world may see God's working in the world and ultimately see his image in the world. It works to transform individuals and the church into His image. And when His church is the image, Christ is revealed, and God is magnified (aka glorified).

Up until now, I have been focusing on mostly the "big picture" of the story of humanity and the progressive revelation of God's image in the world. Of equal importance, this story gives insight into the very meaning of human existence and the life that God calls each of us to. I would like to point out that each individual, on some level or another, is destined to live out the story of humanity in their own life, and every Christian is called to redeem this story of humanity by living out the story of Christ. Every human joins the story of humanity, *created in the image of God*. Every human joins the story of Adam by eating the fruit and failing to be a perfect image of God; from whence we exile ourselves to the wilderness, failing to grasp the meaning of life. We, called by Christ, enter the story of Christ through his revelation to us (his incarnate presence in our life), we join with Christ's crucifixion through a death of our flesh, and we are resurrected with and through Christ as a new creation. We, called to be the new humanity that creation longs for, *with unveiled face are being transformed into the same image from one degree of glory to the next through the work of his Spirit.*[40] *We no longer live but Christ in us.*[41]

We come face to face with the incarnate Christ and he invites us to join with him in being his incarnational presence in the world. We first receive the revelation of Christ through the work of the church and of those apart of the body of Christ. We, then, enter into the body of Christ and partake in being the incarnate presence of God to the world.

In the same way that Christ lived and walked on this earth, the body of Christ continues to live and walk in the path Christ started. We do not move beyond the life of Christ, but we continually live in his death and resurrection through the Spirit's presence in our lives. Continually, we are transfixed into the new creation from one degree of glory to another.

We continually live the life that Christ lived. If we are the body of Christ, then *what Christ was and is to us, we (the church) are to be to the world.* What Christ has done for us; we are to do for the world.

But, if we are to "be Christ" to the world, we must be transformed into his image. Our very character is to be steadily transformed by the character of Christ and made more like him. Our perception of the world around us will change and we will begin to see with the eyes of Christ. This is the call of every Christian. This is the call and vocation of the Church – the body of Christ. *Finally,* we can fulfill what we were made for. The meaning of life is no longer something that is impossible for humanity to achieve. The meaning of life finally fulfills its purpose in that we are able to reflect God's image. *The old is gone, the new creation has come.*[42] And, as Adam rejoiced over Eve; Christ rejoices over his church, *"At last! Bone of my bone, flesh of my flesh.*[43] *You shall be called Christians* (i.e., "Christ-like," or "the people of Christ"), *for you were taken out of and belong to Christ."*

Chapter Main Ideas:

- We were created in God's image to be like him and to be in relationship with him.

- Humanity is sacred in the eyes of God.

- ~~Jesus is the clearest image of God that has been given to humanity; therefore, he is the model for how God intends us to live.~~

- The cross is the exemplary image of what it looks like to bear God's image in a broken world – bearing the sin and ugliness of the world to bring about redemption.

- The resurrection shows us what a redeemed humanity looks like.

- Through the Holy Spirit, we are enabled to be Christ's body to the world by entering into Christ's crucifixion, resurrection, and new creation.

- ~~Finally, we (individually and as the church) reflect God's image – fulfilling the purpose of what we are created for.~~

All of this is
spot on
theology!

3

A PRIVILEGED JESUS IN A BROKEN WORLD

> There was nothing attractive about him, nothing to cause us to take a second look. He was looked down on and passed over, a man who suffered, who knew pain firsthand. One look at him and people turned away. We looked down on him, thought he was scum. But the fact is, it was *our* pains he carried— *our* disfigurements, all the things wrong with *us*. We thought he brought it on himself, that God was punishing him for his own failures. But it was our sins that did that to him, that ripped and tore and crushed him— *our sins!* He took the punishment, and that made us whole. Through his bruises we get healed.
>
> Isaiah 53:2-5 MSG

The calling to be "like Christ" and to be members of Christ's body is certainly a lofty and seemingly unattainable calling. I mean, Jesus is the Great High Priest, the healer of all diseases, the Lord, the teacher, the creator, the mediator, the suffering servant, the sustainer, the savior, and on and on the list goes. This leaves us with infinitely large shoes to fill. Yet, if we are any of these things, it is because of Christ's Spirit (not our effort) in us that allows us to be so. It is an odd dynamic to consider; we must strive to be these things, but if we actually reach our goal it won't be because of our striving. Paul captures this mystery in saying, "Continue to work out your salvation in fear and trembling, for it is God working in you to will and to act in order to fulfill his good purpose."[1] We tremble and fear to live up to Gods calling, but it is God who enables us to do so. This certainly is a difficult concept to grasp logically but is perhaps easier learned through living it (as any philosophy that is not lived is never fully understood). It is only by God's mysterious grace that we are able to share in the Messianic (i.e., saving and liberating) ministry of Christ.

We now share in the original vocation and mission of Christ. We are now to be "Jesus to the world," animated by his Spirit. When we, in the context of privileged, put on Christ there are certain implications for how that privilege will be incorporated into our vocation of "being Christ to the world." First off, Jesus provides us with a stunning and radical picture of what this looks like. For, if anyone was privileged, it was Jesus; for he was God and the whole world could be at his fingertips if he so desired. The way that Jesus dealt with that privilege provides insight into the kind of lives we are to live. We will now explore two broad characteristics of Christ that shed light onto the type of life God calls the privileged to: lives marked by (1) humility and (2) authority.

Part I: Humility, Laying Down Privilege

Pride and Privileges

Those who are privileged find it difficult to be humble and naturally easy to be proud. After all, our success and accumulation of wealth is often attributed to our own abilities, skills, hard work, and spiritual superiority. I have often heard it said that the reason the West has been so prosperous is because of Christianity's influence. In essence, *our prosperity must be evidence of God's blessing.* However, I wish to point out that the Bible seems to associate wickedness with riches far more often than it associates material riches with the blessedness of God. And, those who are poor are often the one's whom the Bible says are on the side of God. In this light, it is almost more likely that *our prosperity is a sign of our own selfishness and past or present oppression of others.* In honesty, our (American) prosperity is undoubtedly the natural result of centuries of free labor via slavery and free land and resources via the conquest of indigenous people.*

Not only is privilege often evidence of past wickedness, it is also often the sign of future destruction. The Old Testament exemplifies this repeatedly in the cycle of Israel attaining prosperity, forgetting God in their pride, and then being exiled via a conquering enemy. As a result, prosperity and privilege was, more often than not, a "curse" signifying nearing destruction as opposed to a sign of "God's blessing."

To be clear, it isn't privilege itself that causes destruction, but it is the pride that comes with privilege which precedes destruction. On the contrary, I contend that *Jesus actually does want us to be prosperous and successful,* but humans are so easily puffed with pride and consumed with selfishness when they are prosperous that they almost never practice such prosperity in the way that Jesus desires. One of the image-bearing qualities of humanity was that they were to be gracious rulers of the kingdom[2] – practicing

---

* To be clear, the USA's history is not all bad. There are many valuable and admirable things to look up to in its history and founding. Yet, to glorify the founding fathers as role models of the Christian faith while ignoring their roles in perpetrating monstrous evils is ignorantly evil in itself.

authority in the way God would. God desires his kingdom to be prosperous, glorious, and full of abundance. However, in sin-corrupted humans, pride warps godly authority into a power struggle that seeks glory for oneself.

Thus, when humans obtain a privilege, their natural inclination is to think they have obtained this privilege as a result of their own merit or genius; or, in an even more sinister turn of the mind, one can interpret this privilege as a sign of God's blessing and therefore think of oneself as having done something to put us "in God's favor" while consequently considering the underprivileged to be "outside of God's favor" due to some sin they committed. As a result, it can become all too easy to justify injustice as naturally just while fostering a lack of compassion toward the underprivileged. Such prideful thinking leads to the idea that humans have the "God-given right" to exercise privilege for their own pleasure and advantage – even if that privilege came at the expense of others. Privilege plays a fiddle with our natural sinful inclinations to puff us up with pride.

Throughout scripture, humility is emphasized as something that is incredibly good and pride as something that is audaciously bad. I cannot emphasize enough how serious a position God takes towards pride. God hates pride and loves humility. *He brings himself close to the humble and puts a distance between himself and the prideful;[3] he actively opposes the proud and looks with favor and is gracious toward the humble;[4] he promises that destruction will come to the proud and promises to lift up the humble.[5]*

One of the main reasons God hates pride is because it prevents his precious created humanity from being all that they were created to be. Pride is probably *the greatest* barrier to Christlikeness. God intends us to be like him and God, at his core, is completely self-giving and otherly-focused. Take the Trinity for example: The Father, Son, and Spirit each bound together in harmony and love, seeking to glorify and adore the other above themselves.* When we are puffed with pride, we become self-focused, and this incapacitates us from being able to share in the self-giving love of God. Just as when Adam corrupted humanity when he tried to elevate himself and become "like God" by eating from the Tree of Knowledge, we corrupt and separate ourselves further from the heart of God when we elevate ourselves.

God seeks to redeem us by reforming our hearts into his image. All the while, pride deforms our hearts and puts us further away from God's redemption. Pride effectively poisons the heart and puts us at odds with the work God wants to do in us.

The Divine Grace of Humbling the Proud

If pride deforms our hearts, our privileged circumstances put us in a precarious position in regard to the dangers of pride. Daniel 4 provides a little illustration to exemplify this:

King Nebuchadnezzar had just reached the peak of his success, power, and "authority" (aka, the peak of privilege). Naturally, his privilege gave him a sense that he was better than others. He impressed himself with his own glory. Then, what happens next is really wild. In sum, God caused Nebuchadnezzar to be driven insane and run into the wilderness as if he were a wild animal. Then, only after all his success, strength, and privilege were taken from him, he realized that if he is every successful or possesses anything,

---

* More on this in Chapter 6.

it is because of God's grace. God deserved the glory for any success he had and if he took this glory as his own, it would inevitably lead to his downfall. After Nebuchadnezzar's realization, God gave him his kingdom back. In essence, once Nebuchadnezzar had learned true humility, he was ready to practice the kind of authority God desired.

Again, as in the story indicates, a place of privilege is a dangerous place to be for it makes us prone to pride which alienates ourselves from God. Conversely, one could say that a place of need, poverty, and even mental or physical illness is a much "safer" place to be for it makes us disposed toward humility which brings us closer to God. Pride deforms and poisons the heart and humility purifies the heart. Pride blinds the eyes and humility opens them. The destructive consequences of pride have been built into the fabric of our existence. God will not work in us to make us more like him if our pride continually pushes him away. And, as we push Christ away, we are setting ourselves apart for self-destruction.

Privilege could be considered a litmus test for whether our heart contains pride; for whenever pride is present, privilege will make our pride all the more prevalent. It is no coincidence that the Bible repeatedly associates the rich with wickedness and pride while associating the poor and needy with humility and God's favor. It might serve us well to stop associating material abundance with the blessing of God. For material abundance can give way to pride which puts us further from God's redemption, while material need can give way to humility which provides room for God to purify our hearts.

And, if that isn't enough, pride blinds us to the point that we don't even recognize pride as pride and then to the point that we don't recognize privilege as privilege. It is so pervasive in a culture of privilege that we don't realize how our privilege is putting us in an extremely vulnerable position to the poisoning of our own hearts. And, we may be so blind that we don't even realize that our hearts are being poisoned – that is, unless God mercifully humbles us by causing us to lose everything that gives us reason to be prideful (but that may only happen if one is lucky or "blessed").

In the Nebuchadnezzar story, God gave warning before he took away everything the king took pride in. Daniel said to him that, though the king was humanly mighty, God had it in for him until he would realize that God ultimately reigns. After all, the people God allows to rule on earth are only tiny little people compared to God. At Nebuchadnezzar's request, Daniel gave this advice: *turn from your sins by living righteously, renounce your wickedness by being kind to the oppressed – only then might your prosperity continue.*[6] The king responded the way many of us do, he listened and probably thought it was a good idea; after all, the king put great weight on the words of Daniel. Yet, he didn't really change his mindset or his actions, and a year later, God carried out the consequences of his warning. Consider Daniel's advice to Nebuchadnezzar as a warning for you as well. After all, *what does the Lord require of you?* Love mercy, act justly, and walk humbly. And, if you are struggling to be humble, ask God to do what he did for Nebuchadnezzar. Let the Lord teach you that the right kind of success and authority can only be practiced from a place of humility.

A Privileged Jesus

It is hard to be like Jesus - especially when you have a lot to lose by becoming like Jesus (maybe that's why Jesus said that it is so hard for the rich to enter the kingdom). Yet, Jesus had more to lose than anyone else: he had eternity in unity with God the Father, yet he refused to sit comfortably in his place of privilege and glory while his beloved creation was experiencing the decay and death that is the consequence of sin. He laid down all that privilege and bore the full weight of our sin to rescue us from our pitiful state. The following passage highlights the way Jesus humbly dealt with his privilege:

> You must have the same attitude that Christ Jesus had:
> Though he was God, he did not think of equality with God as something to cling to. Instead, he gave up his divine privileges; he took the humble position of a slave and was born as a human being. When he appeared in human form, he humbled himself in obedience to God and died a criminal's death on a cross. (Philippians 2:5-8 NLT)

Jesus laid down his privilege and became a servant to humanity. If we are to live the way God desires amidst all our privilege and prosperity, we must have the same attitude of humility that Christ had. In the same way, we are to take on the countenance of a servant. When we are seeking to serve others without any motivation to receive anything on our end, we can know that we are doing it out of the heart of Christ. I am convinced that cultivating this humility should be one of the main starting points of being Christlike – especially for those who are already privileged.

And to be clear, this is no feel-good, cookie-cutter, ankle-deep form of humility. This is a devastating sort of humility that sweats blood and bears the world's sin. One cannot easily *have the same attitude of Christ.*

Surrendering our Rights

Within the privileged church, and privileged society at large, there often seems to be a large concern about "our rights." All the while, "the rights" of the privileged are often not even in the realm of possibility for the underprivileged. There is the ever-lamented-about "sense of entitlement" that prevails in our culture and, not surprisingly, is quite prevalent in our churches. Yet, I am convinced that Christian humility means that we must lay down our rights, not demand them as privileged cultured often teaches us to do.

To be clear, there are appropriate instances in which to "demand one's rights;" but it is rarely the most Christlike thing for those in *privileged* contexts. Such underprivileged positions in which I think it would be appropriate to demand one's rights are in such contexts as incidents of abuse, sexism, racism, and the like. Traditionally, Christian activism has gotten it right when the focus has been on the rights of others (e.g., the struggle against slavery, the fight for the rights of the poor in Latin America, etc.). However, privileged Christian defense of "rights" often centers around protecting one's own rights and advantages. Such examples of this include the fight for the "right" to keep tax breaks for churches and clergy, the "right" to gather in churches during a pandemic that threatens the lives of the vulnerable, the "right" to own a gun, and even the historical "Christian" defense of Southern slavery, segregation, or mass incarceration. Privileged Christians have seemingly lost their bearing by having more concern for preserving their advantage as opposed to laying down their perceived rights for the sake of the disadvantaged.

On the other extreme, some Christians may go so far as to say that there is no such thing as a "human right" and that the desire for justice is misguided. Some may quote the verse, *the wages of sin is death*, to make the point that there is no such thing as "human rights" - Humans, just by being humans, have no right to anything besides death. There is a certain humbling value in seeing humanity as sinful and "unworthy" (as we will discuss later on). But, I fear that many have used this type of thinking to justify or brush off copious amounts of suffering in the world as naturally right and just. But, such thinking forgets the inherent dignity and worth God grants to his image-bearing humanity. Life itself is sustained by God's grace, and a world without human rights is a depressing and God-renouncing world.

To the Christian, there is no legitimate claim to the existence of human rights *in a world without Christ*; for, humanity would be "unworthy." But, in becoming human, Jesus proclaimed humanity as worthy and deserving of life, grace, dignity, and respect. After all, the wages of sin are death *only without Christ*. In Christ, human dignity is precious, and any violation of human rights is a form of dehumanization. And, where we see these rights trampled, we must speak up. But, privileged Christians often make a mockery of human rights when we trivialize "our rights" and apply them to things that have little implication in human dignity. Privileged Christians, by definition, live a life far above what is required for basic human rights, but we often view a comfortable luxurious life as our "God-given right."

But, to bring this conversation to a more challenging level, even as Jesus affirms human rights, he also calls us to lay down those rights – and, even in some cases, lay down our basic rights of freedom and life. But before I discuss that further, I will begin with talking about the "trivial rights" that we may be called to lay down.

The Christian life is, decidedly, one of laying down one's rights. Christ laid down all his rights and we are to do the same. This laying down of our rights happens in everyday examples that may seem frivolous, and in profound ways that will severely change our lives. Perhaps, today, this means that we lay down our "right" to buy a bigger house in order that we may fund housing for the homeless; we lay down our "right" to save for our retirement funds so that we can fund an orphan's college education. We lay down our "right" to keep our lane on the highway and allow someone to cut in front of us during traffic merger. We lay down our "right" to own two shirts so that the one who has none may have one. We lay down our "right" to have the best healthcare in the world, so that we can fund healthcare for the destitute. We lay down our "right" to eat to fullness at every meal so that we can share a meal with others who have nothing to eat. We lay down our "right" to dictate our schedule and end up spending the day helping a person in need get from the grocery store to her home. We lay down our "right" to say a prayer out loud in school, in order not to alienate or make others uncomfortable when our goal is to love them. We give up our many "rights" and privileges because we know that they are not ours in the first place.

Everything we own is God's, and he will hold us accountable to how we use (steward) our privileges and rights. When we lay down our rights of reputation, food, clothing, justice, and even life itself, we do so with a trust that Christ will provide for us in our faithfulness. For, when one relinquishes their worldly rights to Christ, one gains the *divine rights* that come with adoption into God's family and citizenship in his kingdom. And, to be clear, these "divine rights" may not manifest themselves clearly in our present lives.

As children of God, we give up our lives and he promises to return heavenly life back upon us. For *if you try to hold onto your life, you will lose it, but if you give up your life for Christ's sake you will find it.*[7] If we give up our food, he'll feed us with manna from heaven. If we give up our money, he will return on us heavenly riches. If we give up our need for vindictive justice, he will lavish upon us heavenly justice. If we give up our family, he will welcome us into his heavenly family.[8] The same goes for our desires, dreams, culture, and anything else. Only that which we surrender to Christ will we ultimately keep. None of us truly have anything outside of what we give to the Lord on the cross.[9]

Unraveling the Cycle of Violence

When one's rights are violated, the natural response is to retaliate by violating our violator's rights. Violence breeds more violence. The Old Testament (OT) itself mandates: *A tooth for a tooth, an eye for an eye.* This OT ignoble mandate entails an *equal retaliation* that would, at least, prevent the Cycle of Violence from escalating. The problem is that retaliation usually escalates, and the Cycle of Violence continues unhindered. From the eating of the Eden apple to Cain's murder of Abel, down to the crusades, the Holocaust, the World Wars, racism, mass incarceration, to the harsh words you spoke today; violence has begotten more violence and has held the world in its grip. Every violent act is preceded by a causal violent act. Whether it be physical violence, thought violence, or spoken violence, *violence* has held our world captive to a chaos and disorder that threatens the very existence of creation. Violence is inherently destructive and yet self-propagating. This Cycle of Violence has continued since the very beginning up until this very moment. This violence has been *systemic* to the way the earth works. Participation in this violent cycle only leads to death – for, as Jesus said, *those who live by the sword will die by the sword.*[10]

I contend that this violence would have long ago destroyed the earth had it not been for the sustaining work of Christ throughout history. Furthermore, Christ's work is not just *sustaining the world* but is the *unraveling* of the cyclical violence of the world. Jesus himself invites us into this sustaining and unraveling work when he throws out the OT teaching of '*eye for an eye*' and replaces it with, "but I tell you, do not resist an evil person. If anyone slaps you on the right cheek, turn to them the other cheek also."[11] This is a way of living that boldly stands up to the Cycle of Violence and insists that *the violence stops here*. By refusing to take part in the Cycle of Violence, we are taking away its ability to propagate itself; thus, unraveling the systemic power that violence has. Jesus says of such people that they are "*the salt of the earth*" and "*the light of the world.*"[12] We are the salt; salt that sustains the earth and keeps it from rotting from violent degradation. We are the light; light that shows that there is hope and good in this world.

Therefore, when we talk of humbly "laying down our rights," we are talking about a way of life which usurps the unjust orders of this planet. We join with Christ's work on the cross that causes the violence of the earth to implode on itself while creating space for God's creational work to bring about abundant life.

For the Sake of Others

This "laying down of our rights" is not passive or weak. It is just the opposite. Laying down our rights is not the same as laying down and keeping a low profile (though sometimes it may entail that). Consequently, it does not mean that we are to keep quiet and not stand up for what is right. In the context of privilege, there are usually not very many rights the Christian has to fear being violated, instead the privileged Christian must be aware of the rights of those who are underprivileged. We must move on from fears of frivolous rights being violated and turn our attention to those who are truly suffering. We are to "speak up for those who cannot speak up for themselves."[13] As those who are privileged, we don't demand our "rights" out of a sense of entitlement, but we plead for other's rights out of a sense of the image-bearing dignity of humankind.

The temptation of the privileged Christian is to stay distant from the suffering since getting too close to the suffering might cause them to lose their "platform." Yet, the irony of the Christian way of life is that we must plead for other's rights by laying down our own rights and joining the underprivileged in their suffering. The Christian "speaking up for those who can't speak for themselves" cannot do it from a distance but must do it from a place of solidarity and closeness with the suffering. After all, how can we truly speak for and give voice to another person unless we are in intimate relationship together. The privileged Christian demands rights by humbly submitting themselves to the injustices the underprivileged regularly experience. The privileged Christian demands rights by laying down their own rights for the sake of others. This certainly is counterintuitive; yet, is not the Christian way of life foolishness in the eyes of the world?

The world teaches that when someone is being unreasonable to us, we are to shame them and expose them. Christ teaches us that we are to humbly submit to the injustice out of loving solidarity and force the oppressor to come face-to-face with their own unreasonableness. One of the insidious aspects of the oppressor is that they often don't see the oppressed as fully human, but once they see a "privileged person" suffering with the oppressed, the oppressor may be more inclined to recognize the reality of the suffering they are inflicting. When someone is unreasonably making demands on your rights, we are not to "stand up for them" but to "lay them down" and appeal to the oppressor out of human dignity. For Jesus says that *if someone slaps you on the right cheek, let them slap you on the left* and *if someone takes your coat from you, give them your shirt also* [14] and *if someone forces you to carry something for them, carry it twice as long as is required.*[15] We do not even have the instruction to defend ourselves from violence, thievery, and even compelled labor!* Many preachers have said, "now this doesn't mean that we let people walk all over us." But perhaps that is actually exactly what it means (in some

---

* Once again, I wish to emphasize here that I am addressing the privileged in this book. I am not talking about the underprivileged tolerating exploitation without doing anything to change their lot. Such a philosophy that I present here could be harmful if misunderstood by underprivileged individuals and perpetuate the cycle of injustice. For example, the spouse who refuses to stand up for herself would actually be better off standing up for herself – and I believe she would be supported by Jesus in such. Perhaps, a "Theology of Liberation" is more contextually relevant to people in such oppressive and unjust exploitative situations. "The gospel for the privileged" is not an excuse to keep individuals in oppression but is the very opposite of that.

sentiment)!* That is exactly how Jesus allowed his opponents to treat him. Yet, it is not a blind submission to the injustice of those who wish to hurt us. It is an intentional voluntary submission to injustice for the sake of reform. It is a sort of "winning by losing." I feel like this has exemplified by the lives of people like Martin Luther King Jr., Mother Teresa, Mahatma Gandhi, and the Apostle Paul. All these people lost much (in worldly terms), but in doing so brought righteous justice into this world. When we are slapped on one cheek and then offer our other cheek also, we are forcing the oppressor to look us in the eye and acknowledge us as a fellow human before slapping us again. Such suffering is not only redemptive for the sufferer but also has the potential to be redemptive for the oppressor.

I wish to emphasize that these words of Jesus are not *principles* that apply to every situation but reflect the *type* of person Jesus wants his disciples to be. When someone steals our coat, we assume that they are doing so because they need it; therefore, we offer them more clothing that they might need. If a roman officer is tired of carrying their load and lawfully asks us to carry it one mile, we carry it two because we know they could use the hand. To be clear, these are not principles or "laws" that we must keep; since, depending on the situation, we must ask Jesus for wisdom to guide us toward doing the most Christlike thing. To reduce Jesus' teachings to a set of rules to live by is a gross oversimplification. But, by all means, we should not be quick to make excuses because it simply inconveniences us. So,

---

* I also wish to make clear that this doesn't mean we always let people take advantage of others or ourselves and do injustice. There certainly is a time for flipping the tables in holy anger. But, we must be slow to anger and abounding in love. Only with God's wisdom can we know when it is appropriate to turn the tables and fashion a whip.

when do we decide to take the extra slap or not? I say, *when in doubt*, take the extra slap, give away the extra shirt, and carry the burden extra far. It is better to err on the side of humility than to err on the side of convenience.

The Voluntary Nature of Humility

This "laying down" is to be the voluntary act of the Christian – it is not the forced submission of a lower caste individual. When a worldly view of humility persists, humility is seen as weakness. Yet, a godly view of humility reveals it as the ultimate strength. Humility is not the same as humiliation; humiliation is when the vulnerable are exploited for a laugh. Humility is the embrace of situations another might consider humiliating - all for the sake of the redemption and elevation of the humiliated. There is a certain dignity in such a voluntary act that brings redemption to others; and during such an act, those who are oppressors begin to appear all the more undignified. Humiliation causes shame, but humility done in the heart of love highlights the dignity of humanity. Furthermore, the idea that such humility is voluntary entails that that the individual who humbles themselves must come from a position of certain authority, or control of the situation.

Many in Jesus' time must have thought that the crucifixion was humiliating for Christ and that it revealed all his weaknesses. Yet, Jesus had a deep understanding that such humility would indeed be his glory. Jesus alluded to this when he said, *No one takes my life from me, but I lay it down of my own accord. I have authority to lay it down and authority to take it up again.*[16] Christ's surrender gave way to the revelation that he was the ultimate authority – God. Christlike surrender is always voluntary, and this surrender is always aimed at the lifting of those who are not privileged enough to surrender. Christlike surrender is the civil-rights-spirit of laying down one's rights so that the rights of those who have none may be established. Perhaps, we are to allow people to walk all over us in order to keep others from being walked all over. This is a radical laying down of our rights. It is a "dying to ourselves" that we cannot do unless the life and death of Christ is flowing through our being. And, such a laying down is the way that Jesus calls us to love our neighbor, for, "Greater love has no one than this: to lay down one's life for one's friends."[17]

This is what Christian engagement with the world is to look like. Evidently, this demands much humility on our end for it is extremely hard to suffer injustice. Christlike suffering is always voluntary and aimed at the benefit of the disadvantaged.

All the while, we must remember it is Christ to whom we are surrendering. When we come to Christ, we lay down all our rights and responsibilities at his feet. At Jesus' feet alone – not the oppressor, persecutor, or any other "authority." This is why, Paul, while in chains and in prison, doesn't consider himself a "prisoner of the Roman government" but a "prisoner of Christ."[18] Christ is the ultimate authority in every situation. And, if you have suffered injustice in your position, you can be sure that Jesus will eventually make it right. Therefore, even when we are facing persecution and suffering which may seem involuntary, it may ultimately be the result of our voluntary submission to Christ (I presume this is why Jesus told us to "count the cost"[19] before we commit to following him). Furthermore, when we suffer, we may rejoice that we are counted worthy to suffer for his name, for we know that Christlike suffering is always somehow redemptive.

The Foolishness of the Cross

Furthermore, we cannot let ourselves define what this "laying down of our rights" means. It must be defined by the ethic of Jesus. Jesus was God, and God needs nothing from the human race, for everything is already his. If God needs nothing from the world, then his church is to need nothing from the world. The church does not depend on society, or even the laws that govern the land. We need nothing from anything or anyone except from God himself. To think that we need a government to give us our rights and give us tax breaks, we insult God's ability to take care of his own body. A paranoia is sweeping some parts of privileged Christianity that the Christian "rights" will be taken away by the governing laws. But, have we forgotten? When we become Christians, we give up the right not to be persecuted. In fact, we should expect to be persecuted! When we become Christians, we lay down our very lives.

Furthermore, this humility of Christ is one that leads to death, and the passage exclaims, *even death on the cross*! Jesus says that we are to *deny ourselves, take up our cross daily, and follow him.*[20] This is a *laying down* of our life and a *leveraging* of our very lives. This is very countercultural: to deny self when we are told that it is all about the self and to actively take upon suffering when we are told to avoid suffering. As Eastern religious thought such as Buddhism becomes more popular in our culture, people are reaffirmed in their pursuit of a suffer-less life. Yet, any reading of the New Testament should leave you thinking that suffering is one of the major aspects of the Christian life – a necessary one that produces Christlikeness – not just any suffering, but a suffering that may even lead to one's death. Dietrich Bonhoeffer says, "As we embark upon discipleship, we surrender ourselves to

Christ in union with his death—we give over our lives to death. Thus, it begins; the cross is not the terrible end to an otherwise god-fearing and happy life, but it meets us at the beginning of our communion with Christ." When Christ calls humanity, he bids them, "come and die."[21] The suffering and death of the cross becomes the beginning, middle, and end of the Christian life.

The cross of Christ seems to have lost some of its meaning in our world of cute cross necklaces and fancy church steeples. As a result, we often need reminding that the cross was a brutal form of torture and execution. In Jesus' day, the cross was an offensive symbol that represented a bloody death. For Christians to adopt it as the symbol of their faith is to associate Christianity itself with a horrid death. Such an audacious symbol representing the beauty of Jesus' death, and the path that the disciple is to follow in. It is a completely counter-intuitive choice of symbol to represent a movement. Today, it would be like choosing a noose, or the electric chair as the symbol of your movement. Could you imagine if people walked around with shirts depicting a man in an electric chair? Or, necklaces with a noose at the end? It would be offensive and *rated R*. Such is the life that the Christian is called to. In fact, for the disciple taking up their cross is like getting in line for death row. This is Christ's invitation to you; is that what you want? The life of the Christian becomes one of someone who has received the death sentence – we know that following Jesus is the same as us being led to our execution. Every step is a step closer to a gruesome death. But, because the Christian is under a death sentence, the disciple no longer has anything to lose. Surely, to fear death is to fear the Christian life itself. As a result, a goal of every disciple of Christ should be to get to the point where death is no longer feared, for only then is their hope completely placed in Christ and nothing can hinder their walk with Christ on earth.

Jesus says, *"whoever loses their life for me will save it."*[22] Therefore, the Christian may risk all for Christ, for even in death all is not lost – but all is gained! Truly, one who fears death also fears life itself; Yet, with God's view, death seems like a foolish thing to fear. For, we must not forget that this "loss of life" is followed by a resurrection that makes our current life seem like a fading dream. That is why Paul says that he considers "our present sufferings are not worth comparing with the glory that will be revealed in us."[23] Death will surely be the beginning of life for us.[24] When the world sees such people living with this truth in their heart, they will call them foolish and conceited – even some in the church will say such things. The cross is designed to humiliate criminals, but in Christ, the cross is one's glory.

Imagine a sanctuary today where people come to gather every week with an electric chair on stage and sing songs about "the wonderful electric chair." Then they proceed to eat bread and wine, all the while imagining it to be flesh and blood. We would probably consider such people freaks, foolish, or mentally deranged. Yet, that is precisely what Christians do every week. It is certainly strange how we so easily forget how insane our faith is. No wonder Paul says that *the cross is foolishness.* [25] Yet, to us who are being saved, the message of the Cross is *the power and wisdom of God*[26] and *the aroma of life-giving perfume.*[27] Ideally, when we are well-along in our walk with Christ, we will no longer think of the Christian life in such dark terms of *death to self,* but instead only be captivated with the Christian life as *life in Christ.* In reality, every man is already under a death sentence; the Christian is the one who embraces it as a means to glorification.

Mother Teresa as an Example of Humility

There was a moment in my life when I really felt like I understood on a deeper level what humility is and how I could practice it. I had just traveled to India and stayed there for a little over three weeks. God had placed the word *humility* in my mind and my main prayer had become "Lord, teach me what humility is and what it is to be humble." During our time there, it was 113°F (46°C) and we did not have any air conditioning. At night, it would get down to maybe 97°F (36°C). We would go out in the heat of the day and work in a medical clinic for a few hours caring for basic health needs. Through much of my life, one individual that I very much have looked up to is Mother Teresa – a person whose life work mainly consisted in India and whose radical service of humanity changed the world. I have always known that she was considered a "humble" person. But, being in India really showed me what humility she must have had. After just two weeks amidst the heat, pollution, noise, and poverty, I was ready to go home to my comfortable quiet bed. Yet, Mother Teresa left her comfortable life in Europe to live in India. She lived in a gated community where nuns live, but she found it unbearable to be living in such comfort when their neighbors were living in rags.

Mother Teresa would leave the shelter and see the people living on the streets in rags. She couldn't bear to live in her nice house in the midst of such poverty. She requested permission to leave the commune and start another in which the nuns would not own more than the people they served (which was nothing!). In this dusty, scorching hot, polluted place - Mother Teresa embraced humility for the sake of "the least of these." Her team would go out in the streets and find those who were suffering most and were on the brink of death and bring them back to their living quarters and clean their wounds, give them water, and hold their hands while they died. This is not as glamorous as many depictions of Mother Teresa might have you believe. It was sweaty, uncomfortable work, to serve a people that was not their own. To smell the rotting of limbs falling off due to leprosy or to watch the squirm of maggots as they eat away at a wound that hasn't ever been properly cared for. I think of the humility that Mother Teresa possessed, and I am embarrassed that I desire such comfort and healthy living situations simply because of the heat. (In coming back to Canada, I truly felt like I was landing in heaven on earth - clean air, peace, and minimal suffering surrounding me.) But to bear the heat and to do all she did, this could be none other than Christ's love flowing through her.

One could argue that it would be easier to be a martyr than to live such a life - being a martyr might be the easy way out (one might come to that conclusion especially after reading the last section on the cross). Yet, even Mother Teresa's humility does not compare to the humility of Christ. This humility is one that we must learn from. Try this yourself, think of the most uncomfortable place on earth, most uncomfortable temperature, even think of dangerous places - if there's a place you think of, imagine living there your whole life, without worldly comforts, and all for the sake of serving your fellow humans. That is what humility looks like - to lay down one's life for their friends; and when such humility is attained, it isn't much different from love. Jesus left the kingdom to die and suffer as a homeless criminal – rejected. Must we also leave our American mansions and lower ourselves lower than the least of these to lift them up? If we do so, we will inevitably be humbled and rejected as Jesus was.*

Such humility cannot be learned through meditation, reading, or a "focusing of one's heart;" such humility is only learned through practice. Only when we lower ourselves lower than the least of these will we be able to develop a humility in our hearts. Without such practice, humility is only a theory.

The Law of Christ

When looking at the big picture and consider concepts like "carrying our cross," "laying down our lives," "being like Mother Teresa," or "acting justly;" it can be difficult to see how these apply practically to our day-to-day lives and think that we must go out and search for "big ways" in which we can do such actions. But, if we are ever to lay down our lives in big and extraordinary ways, it must start out with a laying down of our lives in ordinary small ways. For, *those who are faithful with little, will also be trusted with much.*[28]

Paul puts this exhortation simply: *Bear one another's burdens and so fulfill the law of Christ.*[29] Jesus himself bore our

---

* Side tangent: I feel like Mother Teresa sometimes gets a bad rap and is largely misunderstood. For one, some people think she didn't do much besides sit with people who are dying. Yet, this simple act of compassion lead to radically transformed lives and the establishment of ministries and organizations around the world that aid the poor. Her simple acts of humility gave her profound authority and influence in the world. Secondly, I hear so many people say, "we can't *all* be Mother Teresa." Of course, we're not all supposed to be Mother Teresa, but maybe you can be your version of Mother Teresa or at least learn from her humility.

sin and the full consequences of our sin. If we are to do the same, we are to bear one another's sin. This means that we are willing to put up with one another's sin, annoying habits, and ugliness. But not only that! We are to be willing bear with others who bear the brunt of other people's sin. This means that we must be willing to say to those around us, "I am willing to enter into your situation and help you bear the consequences of your sin as if they were my own," and, "I am willing to enter into your situation and help you bear the consequences of other's sins that have been placed on you." This is the Law of Christ.

How often do we look at individuals in difficult situations and think, "they got themselves into that mess" and then use that as an excuse for leaving them in their pitiful situation? How often do we think, "if only they weren't such sinners, their lives would be much better… If only they hadn't gotten into drugs, if only they would have held to a Christian sexual ethic, if only they hadn't committed a crime, etc.?" We love to blame the sinner and, therefore, let ourselves off the hook from having to help them. But, we also must admit that the sinner isn't always the one solely responsible for their own difficult situation. Their situation is usually difficult as the result of sins committed against them. And, even if their suffering were solely their fault, the Christlike response would be to help them bear their sin anyway.

Again, the Law of Christ says, *I see how the consequences of your sin have impacted you and I am willing to bear those consequences of your sin with you, nevertheless. I see how others' sins have impacted you and am willing to bear the burden that others' sins have placed on you.*

This is a radical upheaval of our ideas for what it means to love others. How many times have you tried to love someone, and it becomes too difficult and burdensome you conclude that it is just not worth it? We often are willing to help others deal with their life situation – but, only up to a certain point. We may decide that it is too demanding, draining, or simply that we are not getting enough out of this relationship. How many times have we helped someone in need, only to find that they keep coming back to us because they need more? And, as a result, we start looking for ways to get rid of them or ignore them. How quick are we to cite "boundaries" and our own agendas to excuse neglecting the needy? How quick can we be to anger or frustration when our friends or spouses are annoying us, asking too much of us, or are being "needy"?

When we realize that our vocation (purpose for existence) is to bear one another's burdens, perhaps, we will be able to draw from the well of life and find it within ourselves to have patience, compassion, and to go the extra mile. Our whole life in Christ is to model his burden-bearing love for us. Therefore, as far as it depends on us, we seek to put up with and bear the consequences of other's sin as we are animated by the redeeming love of Christ. This means that we do without convenience or even pleasure to bear one another's burdens. The problem is that we often see *love* and *bearing one another's burdens* as a "side project" in our life focus of professional ambition, personal enjoyment, and familial focus. As a result, we see *bearing in love* as something that "gets in the way" of our purpose instead of it being the very thing we live for. When we make *burden-bearing love* the most important aspect of our existence, it becomes much easier to live it out. Burden-bearing love must be our main priority.

We bear other's sin by having grace for other's faults, weaknesses, annoying social ineptitudes, or any other thing that feels like it violates our rights. We have grace and love for others when they beat us, steal from us, or even betray us. We bear the brunt of other's sin because Jesus insists that this is the kind of love that brings about redemption. We visit those in prison who suffer for their sin and we join with others in bearing the sins that they must unjustfully bear - people who have difficulties keeping relationships because they have been sexually abused time after time, the mentally ill that have been abused throughout their lives, the poor that have born the weight of other's greed and discompassion, the diseased who bear the results of a broken and sinful world, and the orphaned who have lost parents in one way or another. We find ourselves amidst broken and, admittedly, difficult people because those are the people Jesus found himself in the midst of – the tax-collectors, the prostitutes, the drunkards, the demon possessed, the diseased, the poor, and the sinners. And it is not just the prostitutes, tax-collectors, and other "sinners" that we must bear sin for, but our very own families, neighbors, and friends that are just as much sinners as any other. To bear sin in all relationships is how the cross of Christ works its way into every aspect of our lives. This is what a humble denying of oneself looks like.

And, we, who are privileged, have been given much more resources and capacity (at least materially) to bear with other's sins than those who have not been given such amenities. We have much and that is why Jesus expects much from us.

The Worst of All Sinners

We, as humans, have all the more reason to be humbler than Jesus himself was. For one, we are not perfect, and we are sinners. Surely, this is an innate humility that we possess that Christ did not. Paul said that this was a trustworthy saying, "Jesus came into the world to save sinners – of whom I am the worst."[30] In context, Paul calling himself "the worst of all sinners" may be a reference to his past life as a Christian killer; even so, I think that this saying of Paul also presents a challenge to the reader to consider how they may also be the worst of all sinners. Therefore, this leads me to this question: Have you ever thought of yourself as the worst of all sinners? Honestly, most of us can think of someone who is a "greater sinner" than we are. Yet, Jesus says that the one who thinks in such a way does not go away justified before God.[31] After much time pondering this, I have been convinced that, on some deep level, we are each responsible for the sins of humanity.

Fyodor Dostoyevsky in his novel *The Brothers Karamazov* writes through one of his characters, "There is only one way to salvation, and that is to make yourself responsible for all men's sins. As soon as you make yourself responsible in all sincerity for everything and for everyone, you will see at once that this is really so, and that you are in fact to blame for everyone and for all things."[32] When I first read that quote, I questioned its truth; but, I kept thinking about it and thought that there is a certain truth to it. Perhaps, the thing that gave me pause about it is that we cannot find our own way to salvation - that was provided by Jesus – who, in fact, made himself responsible for everything and everyone's sin by taking it upon himself on the cross. In the same way of Christ, I am convinced that only when we take personal responsibility for *all the sin* in the world and die to ourselves, we are able to fully follow in the steps of Christ in crucifixion – we *drink of the same bitter cup he drank from.*[33] G.K. Chesterton exemplified this attitude when he wrote a letter to the editor of an article that he read. It said, "Dear Sir: In response to your article, 'What's wrong with the world' – I am, Yours truly, G.K. Chesterton."[34] If this is true, let us develop a humility that can sincerely say, *I am responsible for the evil in the world.*

In claiming responsibility for the sins of the world, we move beyond mere individualistic, personal responsibility into a deeper communal responsibility. The sin of another brother or sister is inevitably *my sin.* In a deep sense, my life is so intertwined with the lives of others that my individuality can never be isolated from the connectedness that exists between humans. This is to be no more pronounced anywhere than in the body of Christ. *If one part suffers, we all suffer; If one part is honored, we are all honored.*[35] And, I do not think it is too far of a stretch to say, *when one part sins, we all sin.* Even so, our individualism tempts us to shirk responsibility and emphasize that we have no responsibility to bear another's sin. So, when someone claims to be harmed by the church in some way, our response is often to say or think something like, "they must not have been real Christians" instead of taking that sin upon ourselves. Over and over again, the church has a hard time doing this.

We often shirk responsibility for the sins perpetrated by members of body of Christ – the enslavement of another race, the fierce defense of segregation, the bloodshed and cultural genocide of the American Indian, and the Crusades to name a few. Truly, these acts were the epitome of unchristian behavior and they must be rejected as such. Yet, we cannot ignore that these injustices were propagated by members of the body of Christ. So, just as Daniel took the sins of his fathers upon himself even when he had no personal involvement of such sins, we must take the sins of our fathers upon ourselves and pray, *"we have sinned and acted wickedly. We have not listened to your word. To us belongs open shame."*[36] Until we truly proclaim that the sin of our father, mother, brother, and sister is our own – no matter how shameful the sin – we cannot bear sin in the way Christ calls us to. Every injustice committed by the church is an injustice committed by me. We cannot stand with the oppressed and say, "I am George Floyd" until we have also stood and said, "I am responsible;" anything less is hypocritical – especially when coming from the mouth of the unoppressed, privileged individual. As we mourn with the hurting, we must also mourn that we are responsible for doing the hurting. This ought to give us a deep sense of humility.

Even in a more individualistic sense, if one took the time to meditate on the depravity of their soul, their perception of the world revolving around themselves, the bad thoughts one has about others every day, and the pride we harbor in our souls – it would probably be enough to convince oneself that they are responsible for the sin of the world. Yet, we have all the more reason for humility when we realize how deeply our lives are inseparable from injustice in the modern world. It is seemingly impossible to get through the day without stepping on someone to live the life we live. For one, much of the food we eat, the clothes we wear, the perfume we use, and countless other consumer products often contain products produced by slave labor conditions. Even if we commit to all fair-trade products, every time we drive a car or throw plastic in the garbage, we are contributing to pollution that is harming the atmosphere which is disproportionally impacting poor communities. Simply by breathing and eating, we may be taking the breath and food away from starving children by misplacing our resources. We choose to buy decorations for our house while ignoring the homeless we pass on the way to the store; I live on land which was colonized through the dehumanizing of people groups and the stealing of their land. The Cycle of Violence is seemingly inescapable; when we participate in it consciously or unconsciously our sins propagate themselves and grip the world around us. How hopeless we are? We are all guilty by association. Surely, I am the worst of all sinners. Worst of all, I know what I ought to do, yet sin in me keeps me from doing such things. Surely, I am the worst of sinners. Furthermore, beyond this logical explanation for why I am the worst of sinners, I am the worst of sinners on some deeply spiritual level. This injustice is unbearable if one chooses to dwell on it. It makes me want to run into the woods and never return; thinking that if I did so, at least I would be avoiding such guilt. Yet, running into the woods would not do any good and I would have no opportunity to contribute to make things right in the world. Jesus came to redeem us, and through us, redeem the world. Therefore, he takes all the guilt from us, he frees us from this sin, and allows us to live a life that makes things right again. Hope.

Perhaps, the first step to making things right and undermining the Cycle of Violence is **confession** – a practice that much of the Evangelical world has forgotten. The Cycle of Violence thrives in silence and the first step to unraveling it is to confess and bring it into the light. The Cycle of Violence also thrives when nobody will bear the responsibility of its sin. There are so many problems in our world today that cannot be pinpointed to any single individual or movement. The problems of systemic and structural violence can seem so invisible to the point that many deny they even exist. Perhaps such sin appears invisible because it is the atmosphere in which we exist. It is like the fish denying the existence of water because they can't see it, but it's the very atmosphere that gives the fish its existence. Although they may seem "invisible," the results of the atmosphere of injustice are evident: starvation, mass incarceration, health disparities, poverty, war, exploitation, climate change, refugee crises, sex trafficking, and the like. These problems that are nobody's responsibility are the responsibility of all. To quote from one of my favorite movies, "when no one is to blame, everyone is to blame."[37]

The first step to unraveling the Cycle is to confess responsibility and participation in it. To bring it into the light so that we can commit to actively resisting it as opposed to passively participating in it.

Confess it with me: *I am the worst of all sinners.* Confess it to one another. Proclaim it on the rooftops. Cry it out while on your knees alone. Confess the specifics of how you have knowingly and unknowingly contributed to the violence in the world. Confess the sins of your brothers and sisters as your own. Confess. Confess. Confess. Bear the cross of Christ, take responsibility for the sin in the world, be crucified with Christ, and live drenched in resurrection hope.

Faithful, not Successful

But, even so, in the process of making things right, we are still bound to make mistakes and end up ignoring others for the sake of the kingdom. A reality where my existence depends on those lower than me is a very difficult reality to exist in. Therefore, I must use my existence to work for those lower than me by lowering myself lower than them.

Although the dissonance is almost unbearable, I think it is necessary for us to dwell on this in order to get a picture of the evil that we are wrapped up in on this earth. Even so, the problems in the world (that I am responsible for) are so large that it seems like I could work my whole life and never make a dent.

A journalist once asked Mother Teresa that very question – "you'll never be able to help everybody, why even try to help?" – Mother Teresa responded, "I am not called to be successful, but faithful." That simple statement has profound theology. In our culture, there is so much emphasis placed on success, and this has seeped into our churches. Too often, we focus on the success of our ministry that we forget the faithfulness aspect of the work. Or, we become so obsessed with results and we think we are failures if we aren't successful. But we are only called to be faithful, the success is up to God. We are the ones who plant the seeds, he is the one that makes them grow.[38] Being faithful has more to do with one's heart than it has to do with the effect one has on the world. Jesus would much rather have us possess a heart that is like his without obtaining success and influence. If we must sacrifice having a heart like Jesus in order to achieve results, then we have completely missed the mark.

So, we can stop stressing about being successful, and leave the results up to God. And if the results are successful, we can take no credit for the success, and only praise God for what he accomplished and that we got to be a part of it.

Humility Comes Before Honor

To take a step back, I'll admit this section of the book was partly a downer, but sometimes we need to be humbled by the gravity of our sin. It is from this point of poverty in which the Spirit that God desires his disciples to persist. "Blessed are the poor in spirit, for theirs is the kingdom of heaven."[39] A consistent pattern throughout scripture is that "humility goes before honor."[40]

Jesus humbled himself to death on the cross; "Therefore, God elevated him to the place of highest honor and gave him the name above all other names, that at the name of Jesus every knee should bow, in heaven and on earth and under the earth, and every tongue declare that Jesus Christ is Lord, to the glory of God the Father."[41] Jesus' humble (and some might say, *humiliating*) death on the cross was the very glory of God revealed to mankind. The cross is the ultimate revelation of the character of God. Jesus, perfect in all manners, united himself with us, in all our imperfection, to bear the consequences of our sin. No one could possibly travel a further distance out of one's way to bear another's failings. *God is love.* Since this humble, burden-bearing love is put on display in the most radical and massive display in the cross, it reveals the character of God more than any other action possible. And, since it reveals God's character so clearly, it is the most glorifying-magnifying event in history. God's perfect love, which is his glory, is put on full display in the cross and in the resurrection is deemed more powerful than death itself.

Similarly, resurrection and glory await those who humbly submit to the cross of Christ, joining with him in his sin-bearing and life-giving vocation. In this, the true character of the new humanity is most displayed and testifies to the glory of the Messiah. Yet, this is not a glory where we are elevated, but a glory in which we get to partake in. And, "we shall be like him, for we will see him as he is."[42] We will behold the glory of the one whose name is greater than any other, and in beholding his glory we are glorified. Jesus is lifted up, crowned king of creation, and everything is brought under his feet and all creation pays homage to him.

> *He gave up his divine privileges; he took the humble position of a slave and was born as a human being. When he appeared in human form, he humbled himself in obedience to God and died a criminal's death on a cross. Therefore, God elevated him to the place of highest honor and gave him the name above all other names, that at the name of Jesus every knee should bow in heaven and on earth and under the earth and every tongue declare that Jesus Christ is Lord, to the glory of God the Father. (Philippians 2:7-11 NLT)*

Part II: Authority, Leveraging Privilege

The Authority of Christ

Within Christ's humility, he also possessed authority that is unparalleled among humanity – he was literally God – the ultimate authority. In this, Jesus could be called the most privileged person in humanity ("divinely privileged"), but, as we have already seen, Jesus did not use this privilege to his own advantage for he laid it down and leveraged it for our advantage.

In reflecting on this, it may seem unfair that Jesus had the advantage of being God. Yet, C.S. Lewis[43] offers us a different perspective with this question: is it unfair for someone to save a drowning person if that person has their feet on the ground? Certainly, we would be angry if someone with such an advantage did not use it to save us. Instead of being bitter at Jesus' disproportionate advantage, we rejoice in the advantage that Jesus has over us because he uses it for our advantage. Jesus' example shows us what it means to leverage our privilege for the advantage of others. Christlike authority is to be practiced by using our positions of authority, advantage, or privilege for the benefit of those who are underprivileged.

The humility of Jesus combines with the authority of Jesus to create a combination that is rare but desperately needed in our world. Contrarily, ego is often considered an essential quality or expectation of the leaders and authorities in the world today. Yet, Jesus was a leader like none other because he was a servant like none other. In the same way, we are called to model our lives after his example of servant leadership.

One of the ways we have been made in God's image is that mankind has been given authority to rule the earth.[44] Therefore, one of the ways we reflect God's image is by ruling – having authority. However, this rule has been warped into the ego-driven oppressiveness that is often seen in authority figures. As a result, the word *authority* is often given a bad rap. We humans seem to misunderstand what real authority is. Often, we see authority as evil, oppressive, or as the big guy standing over the little guy telling them what to do. This is what happens when God's image is corrupted, and we completely misunderstand what God means by authority. Yet, God redeems *authority* in calling his followers into his example of servant leadership.

A worldly understanding of authority replaces a godly understanding of authority. Jesus says, "all authority in heaven and on earth has been given to me"[45] but he did not exercise such authority in the way we humans normally exercise it - he doesn't "lord it over" people. He uses his authority to create a kingdom where the vulnerable lowly are the ones that are looked after instead of the influential wealthy. He uses his authority to heal and forgive. He uses his authority to Love. He models how one is to use their privilege in a godly manner. He used his authority to lay down his life. In a sense, he has the authority to be humble. The lion (authority) and the lamb (humility) become one in Christ.

The Jews hoped their Messiah would wield his authority as the world would - to smash their enemies and make their nation great. But Jesus shows us that such an authority is not as God intended. There is a scene in the Steven Spielberg film *Schindler's List* where a Nazi officer uses his "authority" to shoot Jews whenever he feels a Jew did something wrong. The officer "feels" powerful because he can "deliver justice" with his own hands. Oskar Schindler (the main character) discusses with him that what he is doing doesn't show real power and that real power is found in the ability to pardon people of their wrongs and not give them what they "deserve." The Nazi then goes on to have "mercy" on Jews, by not killing them and consequently pardoning them. Although this was used to manipulate a Nazi into having mercy on Jews, Oskar's words seem to profoundly reflect deep truth as to what God's image of authority is.

God has the authority to kill everyone who messed up on earth (which is, in some sense, what many Israelites wanted); yet, Jesus revealed that godly authority often means having mercy (withholding punishment that is deserved). More so, Jesus reveals that godly authority goes even beyond mercy and into grace (giving a gift though it is unmerited). He doesn't just withhold, but he freely gives all. Jesus shows us what godly authority is – it is to use one's advantaged position to benefit the disadvantaged even though they may not deserve it. In the same way, if Christ's Body is to wield godly authority, we are to lay down our advantage for the sake of the disadvantaged. Mankind was created to rule the earth in a godly fashion, and in doing so, mankind reflects God's image. The authority that is passed onto us (his body) was passed onto us so that we could do what Jesus did with his authority. By possessing and using the authority of Jesus in the same way; godly rule persists; and such godly rule brings about God's kingdom – a citizenry of the new humanity.

A Foot-Washing God

One of the greatest stories of Jesus' humility is in the story of washing his disciples' feet.[46] In Jesus' day, it was normal for one whose profession was that of a lowly servant to wash the feet of the guests after they had been out walking in the dusty and dirty roads. Yet, Jesus (*the Master*) gathers his supplies, and stoops down to start washing his disciples' feet. Peter exclaims, "Lord, are you going to wash my feet?" Jesus says that he is, then Peter responds, "No, you shall never wash my feet." Now, imagine this wherever you are sitting, Jesus walks into your room – Jesus, the creator of the world, the Lord of the universe, the Messiah – he stoops down to wash your feet. Would we not respond the same way Peter did, "Lord, never! If anything, let me wash your feet, though I am even unworthy of that."

The deep meaning of this is maybe a little difficult to understand in our culture since the West doesn't have a very hierarchical culture. It's as if a CEO comes down from his office and starts cleaning toilets for the janitor. Or if you're in India, it's like the highest caste serving an untouchable. Such an act would be unthinkable, as it is unthinkable that Jesus would wash the disciple's feet. It would feel completely unnatural and would seem to disturb the order of the universe. The one who is Lord is serving the one who is the servant. If a servant had washed the disciple's feet, it would have been of no significance, but Jesus washing their feet had significance beyond comprehension. *Jesus' authority gives his service more significance.* What's more, Jesus says, "unless I wash you, you have no part with me."

Jesus can only be our Lord and Savior if we allow him to serve and clean us. When we are following our leader,

Jesus, we are not following someone who lords his authority over us, we are following one who says, "unless you let me serve you, I cannot be your leader." How contrary is this to our thinking in this world!*

After washing his disciple's feet, Jesus said, "You call me 'Teacher' and 'Lord,' and rightly so, for that is what I am"[47] – emphasizing that they acknowledged him as their authority – "Now that I, your Lord and Teacher, have washed your feet, you should also wash one another's feet. I have set you an example that you should do as I have done for you. Very truly I tell you, no servant is greater than his master, nor is a messenger greater than the one who sent him. Now that you know these things, you will be blessed if you do them." If Jesus is our Lord, then we are to use the authority he has given us (as his messengers and image-bearers) to live in radical service of others. Authority is the position that Christ has given us in order to practice humility from. In Christ, the position of authority becomes *the same as* the position of humility.

Before we go any further, I want to stop and take a short detour to reflect on how amazing this is.

We worship a *foot-washing God*. How often do we worship God as a great warrior, wonder worker, and mighty ruler? Such descriptions often make us think of God as this big guy with big muscles, sitting on a throne, or throwing lightning like a javelin. I'm not saying these images are completely misguided, but we also must not forget the image of Christ on his hands and knees, towel around his waist, washing his disciple's feet.

---

* Think of the times when you've been in authority over someone or something: did you use it as an opportunity to serve or to accomplish what you wanted to accomplish?

To further emphasize Christ's humility, the very height of his "wonder working warrior glory" is when he destroyed death in one fell swoop *from the place of a humiliated criminal on the cross*. In his mighty rule, he surrounded himself with promiscuous women of bad repute, tax collectors, and sick people with gross skin diseases. This is a God who allows himself to be seen as a weak criminal with outcast friends who gets on his hands and knees to wash feet. God is a foot-washing God. His self-sacrificial, foot-washing countenance is his glory. We worship a humble, loving, peaceful, nonviolent, self-sacrificial, self-giving, patient, suffering God. *Who on earth has heard of such a God as this?!*

Has not all the world always envisioned God to be a proud, always-right, vengeful, self-glorifying, self-serving, angry, transcendent, untouchable, unhurtable, warrior God? Just read the writings of almost any other religion - or even what some of the Old Testament authors once thought God was like. Perhaps, we have so often viewed God in this primitive way since this is, indeed, how most of us would act if we were given the level of privilege God had (I mean, just look at how the majority of dictators and emperors acted throughout history). Jesus is not the God we would naturally expect. He is a selfless, self-giving God. How radical a God we have - what *good news* this is! Does not such a portrait of God make you want to dance for joy and weep with unworthiness? This God is a God I long to serve, he is not a god who uses his authority to coerce and manipulate me into obedience. He is a God who serves and loves me so much that I cannot help but long to have the privilege of serving and loving him. *Who on earth has heard of such a God as this?!*

Leveraging by Laying Down

Now back to the main discussion of this chapter:

Up to this point, we have discussed humility as a "laying down of our privilege" and authority as a "leveraging of our privilege." As we have already seen, Jesus exemplifies that we are not to practice these two things separately from each other. They are practiced in conjunction with one another. Laying down becomes a mode of leveraging and leveraging is practiced by laying down. Just as we talked about the influence that Mother Teresa's ministry was given through her humility and laying down of her life, if we wish our ministry to have Christlike influence it must start with humility. Humility gives way to authority.

Leveraging *and* laying down; not *or*. I think that one of the main temptations of the privileged church is the desire to leverage without laying down, which is like practicing authority without humility – it comes off as very prideful, ignorant, and, often, harmful. For example, a common mindset in America is that *we live in the best country in the world, the wealthiest, the best educated, and such and such.* And even if it actually isn't *the best,* we are *at least near the top.* As a result, we think of people in other countries as being disadvantaged and oppressed (which some truly are), but as a result we also see them as being uneducated and needy without having anything to offer. Out of this attitude comes the many mission trips that swoop in and assume what needs to be done for the locals, or a belligerent expectation that they conform to the way that we do church in the West. This is what leveraging without laying down looks like. In fact, we need to be going to those countries with humility, considering them better than ourselves, and seeking to serve them on our knees– only then can God's rule begin to spread across the world through us.

What is Authority? A Penny or a Million

As already implied, much of our vision for what it means to practice authority and leverage our positions for the disadvantaged is fairly warped by a *privileged mindset*. For example, we think that we have authority and privilege simply because God has given us more resources. Therefore, when we seek to help those less advantaged than us, we try to use as much of those resources in the most "effective" way possible. No doubt, this is done with the good intention of helping others, but I think our mindsets are completely wrong. Jesus is the one who grants authority and Jesus is the one who determines how effective our leveraging is. Consider what Jesus said to his disciples when they were watching people put money in the offering plate. There was one rich man who gave a *ton of money* out of his wealth and there was a poor widow who gave *one penny* even though it was all she had. Jesus said that this widow gave much more than the rich man.[48] Jesus implies that the widow's penny does more for the kingdom of heaven than the one hundred million pennies of the rich man.

One of our problems might be that we are seeking those who can give out of their wealth instead of those that give all they have. Have you ever heard of a church that would rather have an elderly widow that lives off welfare instead of the millionaire businessman who can pay for a new church wing or even sponsor great mission trips? Has there ever been a charity organization that refuses to schmooze with the rich while going to poor old widows who will gladly give their last pennies for Christ? Our problem is that we think we can accomplish more through those who give out of their wealth instead of those who will give everything that they have. What's more, we often think we are being faithful stewards if we give out of our wealth and consider foolish those who give everything they have. Yet, in Jesus' eyes, the one who gives everything even if it's just a penny to Christ, that penny has more leverage and significance than those who give out of their surplus. If we truly want to leverage our privilege for the underprivileged, we need to stop thinking in terms of worldly resources and start thinking in terms of the heavenly resources that God richly provides when his people are willing to give their lives for him. The widow's penny has more authority and power because it comes from the heart of Christ. The rich man's wealth has less authority and power because it comes from heart of this world.

But, many will still object to the idea of laying down all their resources – and I do too if it is done stupidly. Even so, the one who lays down all of their resources in stupidity probably has a purer heart than the one who hoards most of their resources in the name of *stewardship*. The word *stewardship* automatically brings to mind the parable of the talents; and rightly so: the parable of the talents provides much insight into how we are to leverage our privilege for the sake of others. However, I am convinced this parable has been largely misunderstood and applied in order to excuse what many call "being a good steward." "Being a good steward," meaning, *to save up money, invest, make sure you don't buy a house you can't afford, and paying off one's debt* – pretty much as defined by Dave Ramsey.* All these things are not bad ideas, but the problem happens when we let this define what it is to be a good steward. The façade of Christian "stewardship" and "resource multiplication" is often nothing

---

* A popular self-help financial voice among Christians.

more than a religionized excuse to live more comfortable life.

Jesus is more concerned with multiplying disciples than he is about multiplying resources. But, how often does our multiplying of resources get in the way of our multiplying of disciples? The good steward is one who is faithful with what God has given them and uses it to bring about God's kingdom. We will now turn back to the parable of the talents to explore how this is to look.[49] At the end of the parable, the master rewards his servants who used their resources to create more resources and condemns the servant who hid away the resources until the master returned. He rewards those who were creative with the resources that they were given. We are not called to simply "lay down" our resources, but we are to cleverly use (leverage) our resources to bring about God's kingdom. Although this parable uses the concept of money to make a point, I do not think this parable is primarily about being wise with money; just as the parable of the ten virgins is not primarily about ensuring you keep a good stock of oil to burn. If anything, it is a rebuke to invest one's resources into the things that matter to God. When looked at in this light, the person who puts their money away in a bank is probably more closely in line with the person who buried the money when the master intended them to creatively use it for God's kingdom. Jesus is obviously concerned with eternal investment, not worldly investment.

As if to emphasize what matters to God, the parable of the sheep and the goats is told immediately after the parable of the talents. In this parable,[50] the righteous are the ones who cared for the least of these and the wicked are the ones who ignored the least of these. Certainly, the good steward is the one who uses their privilege for the advantage of the underprivileged – to feed the hungry and thirsty, to invite the stranger into one's home, visit the sick, and clothe the naked. If one is not using their privilege for the underprivileged, it is evidence that will testify against them when Jesus separates the sheep from the goats. Jesus has harsh words for such people, calling them "cursed" and destined for "eternal punishment." Words, that even I am uncomfortable using.

In reality, a good steward is probably considered a bad steward in the world's eyes. The good steward invests in the one thing that has eternal significance – humanity, and particularly, the needy ones of humanity. For, a good steward is the one who sells all they have so that they can purchase the pearl of great value.[51] The kingdom of heaven is the investment that a good steward puts all his resources into. *Store up for yourselves treasure in heaven, for where your treasure is, there your heart will be also.*[52] Is your treasure where moth and rust destroy or is your treasure found in Jesus? It is in the least of these, the outcasts of humanity, where Jesus is found and where Jesus is found is where I want my heart to be. Certainly, God gives us our privilege, resources, and authority for the sake of the underprivileged. He doesn't give us these things as simply a blessing to enjoy;* rather, if we hold too tightly to these things for our own advantage, these "blessings" may easily become considered a curse that leads to eternal punishment.† Leveraging means that we give *everything* (not just some

---

* God certainly *does* intend for his children to enjoy this life, but that is not the primary purpose of this life.
† I do not say these things to scare or condemn, but only to try and get at the heart of what Jesus may be saying – which certainly scares and condemns.

things) that God has given to us for the sake of the underprivileged.

True Authority is Authorized by God

To say that the widow's penny has more authority than the rich man's riches is foolish in the world's eyes. Yet, in the Christian perspective, *authority is only true authority in as much as it is authorized by God.* God created the universe in such a way that love, humility, and compassion* are the real places where authority is present. The moral fabric of the God-created world is composed of love and justice. Therefore, any power that is not built on love, compassion, and humility are destined to fail. *Pride goes before destruction.* Again, we confuse worldly pride and power with authority; but in the Christian perspective, such power is not authorized by God. As a result, any behavior or practice that perpetrates or ignores injustice is bound to be ultimately self-destructive. For, *those who live by the sword will die by the sword,* be it in this life or the next. And, those who lose their life in Christ will truly find it, be it in this life or the next.

Since God built these axioms into the moral structure of the universe, we know that God, love, and justice will have the ultimate say in the universe. This is why Jesus can say that the widow's penny has more authority than the rich man's riches. The spirit behind widow's penny is authorized by God and God's created order, while the spirit behind rich man's riches is not.

---

* Or, you could also say the fruit of the Spirit (aka the evidence of God's presence) here: love, joy, peace, patience, kindness, goodness, faithfulness, gentleness, and self-control.

Called to Take Radical Risk in Radical Times

We often shy away from things that are risky, especially when we repeat the refrain of "being good stewards." Yet, as already discussed in our discussion of the cross, we are called to risk our very lives for Christ; therefore, no risk is off limits to the Christian and no risk is too foolish if done in the Spirit's leading. We must have boldness to take these risks. So, when figuring out how to lay down and leverage your own privilege, perhaps one should go a little beyond what they are comfortable with – we cannot be afraid of taking radical risks. For, in pushing the limits, we will grow and give God a chance to use us.

Furthermore, by taking the risk of laying down everything before Christ we may see Christ's kingdom breaking in on this earth in new ways. Take miracles for example. In the West, it seems very rare for us to see or talk of witnessing miracles. Many of us are disappointed not so see such supernatural interventions. Others of us have grown complacent and don't care to see or experience miracles. And, most of us probably rarely ever ask for a miracle. But, perhaps there is a reason miracles are so foreign to us in privileged Christianity. Perhaps we don't see miracles because we never need them. We always have a doctor to heal us, we always have a savings account to rescue us, and we always have insurance to bail us out. We have become so good at finding our own security that we never need to depend on God. But, once we take risks that are slightly beyond our capacity to handle, such faith will be rewarded with God showing up and providing us with a miracle.*

In a privileged context it is hard to imagine giving everything for Christ when becoming a Christian doesn't necessarily demand that kind of cultural risk. Furthermore, one might think that only radical times would call for such radical risks, and, to risk all for Christ when it is "unnecessary" would be completely foolish. I am convinced that it is not just in "radical times" such as apartheid, the civil rights movement, the holocaust, humanitarian crises, wartime, or other times of mass social evils that call for radical risk-taking in the Christian life. We must re-realize the urgency of the early church and realize that these *are* radical times in which the Spirit of God is poured out on his people and the unjust darkness cries out for justice and light. We must stop ignoring the radical time that Christ has called us in. It seems as if the church often waits until severe persecution before realizing that the Christian life requires radical risk. I often wish I lived in times such as the Underground Railroad or Nazi Germany where I might have the opportunity to live radically for Christ. But Christ calls us to radical living *today*, whether we live amidst radical injustice or not. In truth, every injustice is radical disobedience to God's plan, thus radical measures are required by all Christians at all times. For, "injustice anywhere is a threat to justice everywhere."[53]

---

* In all honesty, miracles have been foreign to me in my walk with Christ. I wish this were not the case, but I confess that I am uncomfortable talking about miracles or even praying for them. Perhaps, that's why I say so little about them in this book.

Even today,* every serious Christian in America ought to consider the merit of smuggling refugees fleeing for their lives from the drug lords across the border into the United States so that they may receive the compassion of Christ. I know even such an idea is extremely controversial, but radical risks in history have often been seen as such (i.e., Christian resistance in Germany during WWII, The Underground Railroad, and even the civil rights movement). I am not saying that this is what Christians are supposed to do, but I am saying that we should consider the injustice in the world and seek to bring justice and the love of Christ despite the risks. Sometimes this might look like smuggling people across the border, other times it might mean providing aid to immigrants who need it across the border, and other times it might mean helping refugees apply for asylum and advocating for legal reform – either way, such actions will be considered controversial by some – and maybe even looked down upon by the privileged Christian community at large. Although it may look foolish, we need to have the courage and Christlike wisdom to think counter-culturally and counter-intuitively in our laying down and leveraging.

Such risks are what the Christian is called to, regardless of the potential dangers. In fact, Paul says that *anyone who wants to live a godly life will face persecution.*[54] A godly life is, by definition, a life that invokes persecution by the powers of darkness. If anyone is a real threat to the devil, they will face an all-out attack from the devil in order to discourage

---

* Today, meaning a time where Trump-era immigration and refugee restrictions have created refugee camps with horrid conditions right across America's border in Mexico. By the time you're reading this, this example may be irrelevant, but I'm sure you can find some modern-day injustice that requires radical risk.

them from belief and living a godly life. If one is not a threat to the devil, one probably need not worry about facing much hardship. (Some might argue that Paul's advice was specific to Timothy's time in history, but I don't think this is the case). If we live a godly life, a Christlike life, we will face persecution. And if one faces persecution for a Christlike life, they can take this as evidence that they are on the right track.

In one story, John Wesley is said to have gone three days without being persecuted and was worried that he may have offended God in some way; therefore, Wesley prayed and asked God if he had sinned and if his heart was in the wrong place. From there, a nearby man picked up a brick and threw it at Wesley – to which he replied, "Thank God, I still have the presence of God with me." In truth, this persecution is to be a source of joy for the believer because it means that one is *counted worthy of suffering disgrace for the Name*[55] May we also find it an honor to be disgraced for Christ if it comes to that!

Furthermore, I would like to challenge the privileged by saying that If one is not risking their identity, their comfort, their happiness, their professional career, their safety, their finances, their reputation, even their very life for the sake of those who live in darkness and are bound by the chains of injustice, then one could hardly be considered a "little Christ." Have you ever risked *any* of these things for Jesus? And how might Jesus be calling you to risk these things? Randy Woodley, A Keetoowah Cherokee Christian leader, states, "People have fooled themselves into believing they can follow Christ and risk nothing. But to neglect to stand up for the rights of the poor and disenfranchised is not simply cowardly – it is heretical. Have we fooled ourselves into thinking that true Christian Spirituality can be developed without taking the risk of losing job security, personal safety, or social status?"[56]

Application

I would strongly encourage you to consider what you are to do with your own privilege and through much prayer, wrestling, and conviction from the Holy Spirit.

How might you practice humility and authority in the privilege that God has entrusted to you?

One way you might do this would be to write out every privilege that you have and consider how you might leverage and lay down those privileges for the sake of the disadvantaged. Make a list of every privilege you currently have. To give you some ideas, we can be privileged in almost anything: culturally, racially, educationally, spiritually, religiously, financially, and in regard to our gender, time, influence, health, safety, security, etc. Or, other times it is impossible to literally lay down a privilege (such as the color of your skin); therefore, we must come up with creative and thoughtful ways in which we can do this. Furthermore, since it is a laying down and leveraging *for the sake of those who have less privilege*, it might be helpful to consider your relationship to those who have less privilege than you do when considering how you might apply the authority and humility of Christ to your life. You might find that you are already practicing this, or you might realize that you live a self-absorbed lifestyle; either way, we need Jesus.

Furthermore, recognizing one's own privilege isn't as simple as sitting down and making a list. It is a process and a wrestling. Often, what makes this so hard is that we don't even realize we are privileged when we really are. That is

why it is so important to have diverse friends with diverse
levels of privilege (more on this in chapter 6). We have to
get out of our own little privileged bubbles. Often, getting
out of these bubbles is one of the hardest and most
uncomfortable parts of this process. And, since we are to
leverage and lay down our privilege for the sake of the
underprivileged, we ought to be in relationship with the
underprivileged. We cannot really do something for the
sake of another unless we really understand their needs and
receive their input and guidance as to what this looks like.

I would also again like to point out that the temptation
for privileged Christians is to only leverage our privilege
without laying it down. But, to leverage without laying
down is un-Christlike. We would rather be distant
philanthropists than incarnate missionaries. You may be
praised by those around you, but it will not result in the
same redemptive change as leveraging by laying down your
privilege would.

It is all God's Doing

After considering the practical applications of humility and
authority, it might be tempting to think it is all up to us to
figure out and decide how we are to apply these virtues to
our life. In truth, however, any humility that we accomplish
is because of Christ's work in us and any authority that we
possess is given to us by Christ. It can be easy to fake
authority by using our position of power to help others and
it is easy to fake humility by just giving away stuff or
stepping aside. But, this humility and authority will lose its
meaning and substance unless it is rooted in the humility
and authority of Christ – not rooted in the cleverness of our
own minds or the laziness of our flesh. Certainly, God gave

us minds for a reason, but we must be sure not to let our minds become "god" by making all the decisions and effectively leaving God out of the decision-making process.

It is through much prayer and petition that we seek God's will for our lives, ask for God to possess us with his attributes, and put our faith in him. Our walk must begin with much time went with God. However, I find that the use of prayer has also been used as an excuse for inaction. For example, "God hasn't told me what to do, so I'll just keep doing what I want until he does." As much as we don't want to admit it, I think that this is the heart that we have much of the time. But, I am convinced that such thoughts come from a heart of unbelief. Indeed, when we pray and ask for God's guidance, we should look to hear from him and discern his Spirit, but also know that sometimes his Spirit may be working in us in ways that are undetectable by the human self. Therefore, when we pray, "Lord, lead me," and then sit around and wait for God to supernaturally show up and lead us, we are quite possibly acting in unbelief. If we ask God to lead us, we must believe that he *is* leading us and our minds. And often, we won't really realize God's leading until we look back, surprised at how evidently he was with us all along.

Often, it is this complicated interaction of our spirit with God's Spirit that leads to much confusion in regard to the Christian life. We are always at risk of acting out of our own spirit and disregarding God's Spirit if we put too much emphasis on our own thoughts, plans, ideas, cleverness, and will. Contrarily, we are always at risk of inaction if we put so much premium on "hearing the voice of God" for certain, receiving a "sign" from God, or the like. Much of following God in our life is living in the balance between the two extremes that lead to human-motivated action and God-motivated inaction. Within this tension, we will know God was working through us if we accomplish anything of eternal significance in our lives. Furthermore, our faith is encouraged and strengthened when we take risks based on belief and God pulls through for us in tangible ways. It is also in these moments that we know that God is working through us to bring about his will on earth.

And, that is why Jesus' message is "good news" for the privileged. An abundant life awaits those who are willing to risk all to serve Christ; for in such a life – Jesus will be more present and palpable. No longer are we choked by the worries of this life and we feel a freedom from possessions and privilege. Privilege often takes much effort to sustain, but what free, care-free lives will we begin to live when we lay those privileges at his feet. Just as much as Jesus came to bring freedom to the poor and needy, Jesus came to bring freedom to the rich and privileged. If anyone is poor and needy, oppressed, and lives in a constant state of underprivilege, that is the objective evidence that there is evil in this world. An evil that is systemic and saturating this world. But, freedom in even such a world can be found in Jesus. One teacher says, "Love for those who live in a condition of objective sin demands that we struggle to liberate them from it. The liberation of the poor and the liberation of the rich are achieved simultaneously."[57] Let us struggle with and join the underprivileged – in such we will both find freedom.

Summary: Humility and Authority as One

Humility is the posture of the heart which is revealed in radical service of others, genuinely seeing others as better/more worthy, gentleness, the fruit of the Spirit, lowering oneself below others, laying down all of one's rights and privileges, radical embracing of others (no matter how "disgusting" they appear), non-judgement, no need of recognition, a desire to elevate others, simplicity, perseverance, single-minded obedience and devotion, and unashamed servitude.

Humility is contrasted by cleverness, entitlement to one's rights, jealousy, isolation from others, avoidance of suffering, and a hunger for glory and recognition.

Humility is a laying down of one's privilege for the sake of the underprivileged.

Authority is the place God grants to us for the purpose of practicing Christlike humility. God grants every human authority since they are made in his image and are created to co-rule with him. This authority is the freedom to make choices that effect ourselves and those around us. The privileged, by definition, have more freedom and choices that they are allowed to make - often at expense of the number of choices the underprivileged are allowed to make. Therefore, by no merit of their own, the privileged possess more worldly authority.

To the Christian, Christ grants additional authority to be his Body and representation to the world. And, not only that, but the Christian is also given the authority of God's presence. The Spirit grants authority, not on the basis of one's privilege, but on the state of one's heart. Therefore, the penny of the poor widow has more authority than the millions of the rich. Only out of a humble, soft-to-God, and soft-to-man heart, does God's authority do its redemptive work in the world.

Authority is the leveraging of privilege for the sake of the underprivileged. And, to the Christian, this leveraging must be done by means of laying down. Therefore, authority and humility are united as one in the Christian walk. Authority without humility is worldly power and humility without authority is worldly humiliation. But, in combination, they are the power and glory of God. The lion and the lamb lay down together.

4

THE GLOBAL CHRISTIAN

"And as for the outsiders who now follow me, working for me, loving my name, and wanting to be my servants... They'll be welcome to worship the same as the 'insiders,' to bring burnt offerings and sacrifices to my altar. Oh yes, my house of worship will be known as a house of prayer for all people." The Decree of the Master, GOD himself, who gathers in the exiles of Israel: "I will gather others also, gather them in with those already gathered."

Isaiah 56:6-8 MSG

The Anti-Beatitudes

One of the difficulties of privilege is that we do not often recognize our own privilege while it is all too easy to recognize those who are more privileged than us. Therefore, we are often caught in a cycle of comparison which leads us to think we are always somewhat underprivileged or, at the very least, are not "privileged." We either get caught up in the race for what's bigger and better, or we comfort ourselves by saying, at least I'm not living as extravagant a lifestyle as my neighbor. But, this natural tendency to compare is rarely applied in such a way in which our lifestyles are compared with the standard of Jesus. Perhaps. The ignorance of one's privilege comes from the very people that we surround ourselves with and compare ourselves to. We often go to churches and live in neighborhoods with people of roughly the same economic, social, and racial class. Because of this, we rarely come into contact with those who are significantly underprivileged compared to us. And, those who are more privileged than us are the ones we notice.

Furthermore, the Western world has developed a "culture of privilege" in which many feel entitled to spend their lives curating their privilege and comfortable lifestyles. This is perhaps best captured by the term "The American Dream." This is a culture that highly values safety, security, nice house, nice families, nice vacations, nice everything, and, this, all the while living in a nice neighborhood sheltered from the woes of humanity.

One time, Jesus listed the people who were "well-off," blessed, and had it good in this life. This is usually referred to as "the beatitudes" in Matthew 5. I am, by no means, the first person to state that a "culture of privilege" has the exact opposite values of the beatitudes of Jesus, but I still wish to emphasize this here in reflecting on the "anti-beatitudes"*:

Blessed are the rich (as opposed to poor in spirit):
> We admire the rich and we long to be like them. We live in one of the wealthiest societies to ever exist in history.

Those who laugh (as opposed to those who mourn):
> We admire those who have "light hearts" and are always laughing and having a good time.

The accomplished people who can steal the spotlight (as opposed to the meek):

---

* Yes, it's kind of corny, and I've seen this way too many times. But, it still gets me thinking.

We admire those with charisma who have accomplished much in life and have been willing to shine the spotlight on themselves in order to get ahead.

The well-fed and spiritually satisfied (as opposed the hungry and thirsty for righteousness):

We admire those who are content and satisfied with living a nice life. We live in a society that has more "spiritual resources" (i.e., books, music, sermons, etc.) than any other on earth or in history. We can easily "get our fill" of spiritual content.

Those who consider themselves better than the underprivileged (as opposed to the merciful):

We look down on the homeless, those on welfare, the "druggies," and those that live paycheck to paycheck. We have little mercy for them.

Those who are the proud (as opposed to the pure in heart):

We admire those who are self-confident and self-reliant. We think being "proud of ourselves" is a very important attribute.

Those who win debates and prove themselves right (as opposed to those who make peace):

We admire those who win arguments and defeat opponents (especially when it's an apologist versus an atheist). We cheer on the victor when Jesus desires us to be peacemakers instead of trying to win a debate.

Those who are popular (as opposed to those who are rejected):

We admire those who are popular, well-spoken of, and have good reputations.

All this is not to say that anyone with privilege cannot be blessed, but it is to say that our privilege does not mean that we are blessed. We are blessed when Jesus proclaims us to be blessed. Either way, this warped idea of what it means to be "blessed" pervades much of our thinking and we admire the privileged and those who have gained privilege through ambitious cleverness. The values of Jesus completely flip upside down the values of the Privileged World.

A Kingdom with no Borders

Even though the values of Jesus are opposite to the world's, the values of our "culture of privilege" seep into the church and pervade much of the thinking that motivates privileged Christians. At any time in history, the church is at risk of being compromised by the values that the culture holds dear. This compromise results in the church failing to be the body of Christ portraying the Image of God to the world. This has happened continuously throughout church history. Specifically, in this very moment, I believe the compromise that needs to be clearly addressed is our value of privilege and position that we are unwilling to give up for the cause of Christ. This reveals itself in many ways, but I think one of the main ways this reveals itself is in the exclusionary ways in which we consider ourselves better than others due to our privilege.

In America, and the West in general, one of the core ways our prideful privilege reveals itself is in the form of nationalistic, ethnic, and/or cultural pride and superiority. Much more could be said about nationalism as I think it is one of the largest corrupting influences on the privileged church, but I will keep it simple. We often consider our possession of privilege as evidence that we are better than the underprivileged when it is more likely to be evidence of barely anything more than the circumstances into which we just so happened to be born into. Ironically, we then begin to take pride in our place of birth – *I was born in the USA, I was born into a family and culture that was "civilized" and learned, I was born in the most powerful country on earth.* And, it is in this pride of culture and birth that has justified and led to many of the horrors of history: colonialism, slavery, genocides, and wars. The belief in cultural or nationalistic or, dare I say, racial superiority (also often known as "being patriotic") corrupt Christian religion to the core.

One teacher says it succinctly, and points us toward a Jesus-centered understanding of nationalism:

> One way or the other, we all think we are the center of the universe because of our place in life. We had absolutely nothing to do with our birth. Jesus did, and He chose a most unlikely city to call home. He was not ensnared by the flimsy and fickle attachments of nationalism.[1]

And this place that Jesus chose as his hometown was Nazareth in Galilee - a place where people asked, "*Nazareth! Can anything good come from there?*"[2] and "*Galilee? Look into it, no prophet ever comes from Galilee.*"[3] By choosing a humble place to come from, Jesus revealed that the place of origin does not matter, but what matters is the place one has in the kingdom of heaven. He also strongly stands against many forms of nationalism. In his day, Jesus stood against the nationalism of his own people that wanted to throw out the Romans that were oppressing them. Jesus taught that we lay down national interest for the interest of the kingdom. He asks us to see our citizenship in heaven as our eternal home that we are to focus on, while our citizenship country is secondary.

In Christ, "there is no Jew or Gentile,"[4] and I could assume we may also say, "In Christ, there is no Mexican or American" - we are all made one in Christ. Our interest is no longer the interest of our country, but the interest of Christ. And, the interest of Christ is much more global and expansive than most of us have been taught in our churches. Even still, this global perspective is not natural for humans; what is natural is an emphasis on our own "identity group" which we tend to define racially, nationalistically, and socioeconomically. And, what is happening to "White privileged Christians" is that it appears that they are losing power in the culture and as a result they/we are becoming more defensive and combative to the groups that appear to lessen the power, strength, or identity of our group. But, the fact that we get defensive over issues such as immigration, shows that we have based our identity too much on our whiteness, English language, or priviledgedness. Our church (especially in America) has lauded patriotism for many years to the point where allegiance to one's country is almost equated to allegiance to God. This is a complete reversal of priorities. Sure, one can serve their country and it be pleasing to God, but if pleasing God is not the first priority, then we have lifted country above God. As Christians, we insist that *Jesus is Lord.* And in doing so, the Christian proclaims that they have no other Lord. Therefore, we cannot pledge absolute allegiance to another. Not to country, not to flag, not to wealth, nor even to family. Christ is Lord, and no other takes precedence (it makes one wonder whether it is appropriate for Christians in America to say "the pledge of allegiance"). Therefore, our identity as a member of Christ's family becomes the identity we tie ourselves to, and, if need be, we cut ties with other identity groups if it gets in the way of our identity in Christ's family.

Jesus himself transcended the nationalistic Jewish culture that he was raised in. In the same way, we are to transcend our nation and proudly take up the banner of a nation that is much greater than any on earth - a nation whose citizenship is founded in God's Spirit living in us. "We are a royal priesthood, a holy nation."[5] In this, we are familiar with the idea that we are supposed to represent Jesus to the world. But, just as much as Jesus represented humanity to God, we are also now called to represent humanity to God. Jesus interceded for all of humanity, and now we are called to intercede for the whole of humanity.

If our interest only lies for those within our own borders, we run the risk of missing the big picture God intended for the church. Therefore, we are to care for our global family with much more care than we do for our nationalistic family. In America, we grieve a death or two of an American overseas, yet we are ignorant of the thousands of fellow citizens of heaven that are being killed for the kingdom of Christ. The Catholic El Salvadorian family fleeing drug wars is as much the family of God as the White Christian we stand next to at church. Yet we seem to care more for the nation's interests than we do for the interest of the kingdom. Worse still, we mock their suffering by calling little things we experience "persecution" or by inciting fears that the Christian in America/Canada's freedoms are going to be taken away and that our rights will be violated. Every little thing is called persecution; we are not even worthy to call our struggles suffering! I do not need to go on, but I will!

Depraved Indifference

Eric Ludy talks about "depraved indifference"[6] and gives us a thought-provoking example of how we should feel about people all over the world. He says, imagine if your child was somehow abandoned in a slum in a dangerous place on the other side of the world - you would do anything you possibly could to save them and make sure that they are taken care of. You would spend all your life savings, break through every wall, ask everyone you know to help you, and more. You would not stop until your child was safe. Yet, even today, there are millions of orphans around the globe that we never take notice of; but, Jesus himself says that *if you give a glass of cold water to one of these little ones, you are giving it to him!**[7] Jesus - the one we Christians proclaim our whole lives as dedicated to - is suffering, starving, and dying. Should not we much more care for Jesus! Would we stop at anything, to see Jesus (our Lord) be taken care of? Yet, this "depraved indifference" prevails when we choose not to think much about it because it makes us uncomfortable or, worse still, we are uninterested in meeting our Lord in his suffering.

On the other hand, I must be honest that we would be completely overwhelmed if we thought this way all the time. We may even go insane and be unable to do anything of meaning if we let our minds continuously dwell on how Jesus suffers throughout the world. Yet, we ought not use this as an excuse to ignore Jesus' suffering! Perhaps we ought to allow ourselves to go insane for a bit and cry out lamentations to God because *there is no way we could save everyone*. But, there is a time to lament and a time to act; as

---

* This might be slightly out of context here, but I think it still applies.

with most things, there must be a Christlike balance between the extremes of indifference and insanity.

This generation is potentially more guilty of this indifference than any other generation in history. Indifference is often an un-Christlike coping mechanism we use to deal with such overwhelming suffering. Before today's technology, much of the world lived in ignorance to much of the suffering that goes on in the world now. Now that we are not unaware, I believe we are called to be a global church more than ever, for it is more possible than it was before in all church history. Just as Paul asked the church in Corinth to give to the church in Jerusalem because they were having difficulties,[8] perhaps Christ is asking us to give to the churches around the world because they are having difficulty - instead of spending it on fancy sound equipment, new carpet, tapestries, media campaigns, or even politics.

We have no excuse now for passing by our neighbor, suffering on the side of the road. Everybody knows of the thousands suffering, starving, and dying of disease; yet, we still try to play the ignorant card. Even our media outlets help us by focusing on news stories that happen in the Privileged World while ignoring the suffering that goes on around the world and in even the impoverished neighborhoods of our very nation. This is an incredibly difficult problem, and it seems much easier to ignore it, give a few dollars maybe, and go on living our comfortable lives in distanced indifference.

We dissociate from the problems in our world, for if we really thought about them the way that Christ thinks about them, then we would have to do something about them. But, if we keep our distance, we can feign ignorance. It is time the Christian church stop feigning ignorance and quit making the excuse that "we have our own problems here" to excuse global inaction. We certainly do have our own problems, but that doesn't give the excuse to ignore problems elsewhere.. Caring for those in the church's neighborhood should be a given (which, sadly, it often isn't). The church loses integrity when they fail to care for the problems in their own neighborhood. What makes this worse is when the church ignores problems in their own neighborhood and still uses the excuse of "we have our own problems here" to get out of having global concern.

Furthermore, the church loses its integrity if it neglects the underprivileged in their own neighborhood while focusing their efforts on those far away. Though, such a way of action is tempting. It is much easier to help people from a distance – we like to send our money and a special few to help the poor in other countries, but when poverty knocks on our very doorstep, we become uncomfortable and defensive. Just bring up welfare or aid to the homeless and you'll no doubt get some people rolling their eyes in seconds. To be a global Christian means that we care for the needs on our doorstep as well as the needs of the world.

Again, it is easy to help people from a distance. But when we come face to face with those people, we become uncomfortable and don't like it very much. It is easy to see a problem and then think - "oh, I can't do anything about that." But the reality is that we usually can do something about it and when we acknowledge that, we are left with this uncomfortable truth. And, when we do think about this issue, we are often overwhelmed by the gigantic problems in the world. We ought to dwell on the overwhelming need in the world and allow Jesus to show us he wants us to invest - all the while, knowing that we *will never* be able to solve it all. We are *called to be faithful, not successful;* to be faithful to do what we can – and what we *can* is usually quite a bit more than we expect.

We who come to Christ ought to seek to expand our capacity for caring for the poor and needy. And, in the case of ourselves (who are overwhelmingly privileged), we ought to use our resources for the advantage of anyone who is less privileged – whether they be in our own neighborhood or across the world. We have the means to help those in our own neighborhood *and* those across the world; therefore, we have no excuse for inaction and indifference. And, if our walk is marked by indifference to the suffering in the world, our walk is marked by indifference to Christ himself. *Lord, have mercy on us and open our eyes.*

The Trap of Privilege

Ironically, it is our privilege that usually holds us back from helping the underprivileged when the very reason we have privilege should be to use it for the sake of the least of these. For example, imagine actually taking a homeless person into your home for the night or even just a meal; what are the excuses that first come into your mind? Here are some common excuses:

- It'd be a hassle.
- I don't want to have anything stolen or broken.
- I don't want to put my family in an unsafe situation.
- I don't have the time.

Now, all of these are valid to some extent. But, they also reflect a certain standard of living that one is unwilling to sacrifice. We don't want our "valuables" stolen, so we don't let the homeless into our home. But, what if we didn't have valuables for the homeless to steal? Then we wouldn't have that fear anymore. Our privilege of owning valuables prevents us from helping the underprivileged who have no valuables. Or, how about the first excuse of not wanting to be hassled or not having the time? Think about the homeless person; how much more of a hassle is it to be homeless? Our privilege of being in control of our schedules and being able to avoid hassle prevents us from helping those who don't have the privilege of a hassle-free schedule. But, what about safety? Surely, if there is a valid excuse, it would be this one. But, even safety, we should be willing to give up for the sake of those who have no safety. How much more unsafe is it for someone to be on the streets or out in the cold? Perhaps we could sacrifice a bit of our safety to provide shelter to the vulnerable.

Yet, my dismissal of these excuses does not mean we throw wisdom out the door. We need to take precautions that we are not putting ourselves or others in overly vulnerable positions. And I am not saying that all people should take the homeless into their homes; I am saying that those who have the means should stop using the above excuses to immediately write off this possibility. Perhaps, it should be the norm for people who have an extra bedroom in their house to allow someone vulnerable into their homes; and only in extenuating circumstances we do not. But the problem is, most privileged Christians probably think that their life situation makes them the exception to the rule. If anything, we should not allow our very possession of privilege keep us from helping the underprivileged. When we start using privilege to excuse oneself from helping the underprivileged, we can know for certain that, for the sake of our own hearts, we need to lay some of that privilege down.

Compassion: Common Suffering

We are called to compassion. The word *passion*, in its old usage, meant "suffering" - that is why we called it "the passion of the Christ." We are called to such a passion as Jesus', and in considering the weak and the least of these, we are called to have *compassion* - which is much deeper than "I had compassion on him, so I gave him a granola bar or a ten-dollar bill." Compassion does not merely mean *pity*. Compassion is a sort of communion one is called to have with the poor - "common passion" or "common suffering." We are clearly called to share in the suffering of the weak. We *share each other's burdens, and in this way, we fulfill the law of Christ.*[9]

One time I was walking with my brother on a rocky path. He had sandals and I was barefoot and being careful with my steps. My brother turned to me and said, "Do you want one of my sandals?" We then each walked with one sandal each - me, better off than I was and he worse off than when he began. But, in compassion my brother was willing to share in my suffering for my good. This example is petty compared to other radical forms of compassion, but it simply exemplifies that compassion is a form of laying down our privilege for the sake of the underprivileged. It is a type of *common suffering* that is redemptive and transforms both the giver and the receiver into individuals that are more at home in the kingdom of heaven. Compassion is not merely taking an hour a week to feed the homeless. Yes, these consist of some of the aspects of *compassion* as the word is used today, but to really have compassion, we must share in the sufferings of those we serve. Perhaps this means we spend a night on the street with the homeless (woah), or better yet, invite them into your home. Surely, *you will suffer*, but the suffering is often evidence of Christlike compassion.

Again, the gospel doesn't call us to mere charity toward the suffering poor; it calls us into friendship with the poor. It calls us to cast our lots in with the poor and for our fates to be tied to the fate of the poor. The gospel is a commitment to identify with the poor and weak things of this earth. We have become deceived to think that *charity* and, even, *generosity* are what privileged Christians are called to. Certainly, these things are good, but they are not the whole gospel. And, too often, we use our *charity* to distance ourselves from the poor or to excuse our neglect of the poor. *Charity* is, too often, the giving of crumbs to "dogs" under the table when we are called to share a meal with the Christ suffering before us.

If we have yet to suffer on the same level of those we serve, then we have not yet lived Christlike compassion. This is radical, unbelievable, and seemingly impossible for the average person to entertain such thoughts. Perhaps, this is why Jesus said, *it is harder for the rich man to enter the kingdom of heaven than to go through the eye of the needle*[10] and *Woe to the rich*[11] because they are comfortable, and it is much harder to give up comfort when one has it. And *Blessed are the poor*[12] because they have not been corrupted by the comfort of wealth.

In the Privileged World, we have considered material wealth to be a blessing from God, but according to these words of Jesus, they may be more of a curse than a blessing! Furthermore, A.W. Tozer says, "If the rich man enters the kingdom of God with difficulty, then it is logical to conclude that a society having the highest percentage of well-to-do persons in it will have the lowest percentage of Christians, all things else being equal," but, historically, "on the North

American Continent, Christianity has become the religion of the prosperous middle and upper-middle classes almost entirely; the very rich or the very poor rarely become practicing Christians." [13] Perhaps, it is time to re-evaluate our faith to determine whether we are correct to place such high regard on success and prosperity. Surely it is possible to be rich and be a blessed Christian for "anything is possible with God." But, at the same time, remember Jesus' words - *blessed are the poor, woe to the rich*.

Sell all you Have?

Jesus said to the rich ruler, "If you want to be perfect, go, sell your possessions and give to the poor, and you will have treasure in heaven. Then come, follow me."[14] This is often interpreted as Jesus choosing the thing that has the hardest grip on the rich man's heart as a test to see if the man would value Jesus over that; truly, I think this was probably Jesus' intention. But, what if Jesus is also speaking to the rich person's ability and responsibility to help those who have less? Jesus highly values justice and helping those in need. Half, if not more, of Jesus' ministry, as recorded in the gospels, seems to be healing the sick and feeding the hungry. Perhaps if we are to be Christlike, we are to also share in the kind of life he lived. Further, Jesus goes so far as to say that *anyone who does not give up everything they have, those who do not renounce all he has, or those who do not give up all his own possessions cannot be his disciple!*[15] Did you hear that? "***anyone*** who does not give up ***everything***..." and that's Jesus talking to a big crowd, not just select individuals. That seems fairly straightforward, and I think that it is time we take such statements a little more seriously and consider that Jesus might actually mean what he is saying.

I am not saying that it is wrong to be rich. I am just saying you must have heard a voice from heaven telling you it's okay to keep an abundance of material possessions because we already heard a voice from heaven saying that it isn't. Blessed are the poor, for they do not have to hear such words from Jesus and feel the same uncomfortability that most privileged Christians have when reading these passages.

John the Baptist's call to repentance was, "those who have two shirts should share with the one that has none!"[16] Although we don't see many people walking around shirtless, I think this statement easily extends to any other issues regarding basic need or human dignity. For example, this begs the question, *is it wrong to possess more money/possessions than another person?* Those were the very words of John and Jesus, and they both walked the talk. They lived lives void of many possessions and without places to lay their heads.[17]

We, as a church, need to think deeply about this issue, and not just gloss it over with "it is the heart that matters" or "it only matters if these things are an idol in your heart." In an ironic way, when we do this, we may be doing the very opposite of what the Pharisees did: They cleaned the outside, but didn't clean the inside.[18] Now, we often think we make our insides "clean" through praying a prayer, and yet neglect our outsides in regard to our salvation. But, if our insides were truly clean, our outsides would reflect this as well. We cannot say that "it is the heart that matters" without expecting the heart to reflect in the way one lives their life. We must "first clean the inside, *then* the outside will be clean as well."[19] Maybe if our outsides do not reflect these values of Jesus, then our insides haven't really experienced the cleansing power of Jesus either.

What are we to do then? Does God really mean that we are to sell all we have? Maybe… But, that is between you and Jesus. I only ask that you talk over this matter seriously with Jesus. Such statements in the Bible entail that we ought to seriously consider the ethics of gathering money in one's bank account. Is it okay to own more than another human being? Should we be saving for retirement when the money in my savings account could be used to feed the poor? Up to what point can we stop caring for the suffering? Surely, I cannot relieve it all?

Surely, this isn't a law or command that we are to sell all we have to the poor, but Jesus came to make us into the type of person who, upon seeing another's need, would not hesitate to give all one's possessions away to help. If we start to consider these teachings of Jesus as laws that we must live by instead of exemplifying the type of person we are to become, then "giving away one's possessions" might turn into another form of legalistic phariseeism. If we learn to live in Jesus' way of love, we won't need to "know all the rules." *For the entire law is fulfilled in this: Love your neighbor as yourself.*[20]

Really? Sell all we Have?

In light of Jesus' call for us to "renounce all we have and give to the poor," a very difficult (and perhaps unanswerable) question appears: where are we to draw the line of caring? It seems that we could care for the poor to the point of giving up all we have and unto death. Surely Christ does not expect me to give up my life for the poor? Perhaps he does. For, Christ was the Messiah because he suffered and died. Are we not called to follow in his footsteps? But, is such a lifestyle sustainable? Still, *why worry? He takes care of the sparrows, will he not care much more for you?[21]* But, wouldn't it be more effective to invest and grow our wealth as a means to continue doing our kingdom work? Does not God call us to be smart with our money?

First, we are not called to be effective; we are called to be faithful - the effectiveness is in God's hands. Secondly, isn't it much smarter to put money into the places that God already told us are good investments rather than risk storing up treasures on earth that rust and decay? *

Another scene from the film *Schindler's List* provides a starting point that is worth touching on. Toward the end of this movie, Schindler had just saved 1100 Jews from being put into death camps by buying them from the Nazis for use in his own "work camp." Schindler has to flee his "work camp" to avoid being caught by the allies and tried as a Nazi. But, before he leaves, he says goodbye to the Jews he saved and his close friends in that group. The Jews present Schindler with a gold ring which said, "whoever saves one life saves the world entire" in Hebrew. Schindler then looks around at everyone and starts shaking his friends' hands goodbye. Yet, as Schindler is shaking hands, he says through a sorrowful voice, "I could have got more out," and starts weeping. If only he had made more money and not wasted so much of it. He looks over at his car and questions why he kept the car – selling it could have saved ten more

---

* There is something good to be said about being wise with money and creating more wealth that could be used for God's Kingdom. But, I feel like this is used way too often as an excuse to hoard safety and security for one's self. Some even deceive themselves into thinking they are applying godly wisdom in regard to money when, instead, it is selfish motives that are applied.

people. The gold pin on his shirt, at least one person. One person is dead because he kept that pin. He weeps into the shoulders of his Jewish brethren – *he did not do enough.* They remind him that they are alive because of him, and there will be many generations alive because of him. But, the emotion is palpable and seemingly unrelievable.

When we consider the actual price of the things we own and how those resources could be used to save and serve others, how foolish do we seem? How many of us will get to the end of our lives and also say, "I could've done more… the car, why did I keep the car?," or, "Why did I spend all that time on pleasure? I could've spent that time with Jesus on the streets." What's more, Schindler *did* spend his entire life savings and risked death to save those Jews – and, still, he regretted so much. How much more will we regret our life choices if we don't even make half of the sacrifices that Schindler made – and that, for life-eternal, not just our present life. *Lord, would you give us a perspective that comes from you. That we may learn to give all we have to you for your work on this earth instead of hoarding it and wasting it on pleasure.*

Pleasure and Suffering are both Necessary

As a disclaimer, I should also note that Jesus said that one should chop off their hands and gouge out their eyes if they caused one to sin. No one really takes this literally, but it emphasizes that we are to be very serious about dealing with sin. However, if we do not take that literally, what keeps me from taking what Jesus said to the rich literally? However, I do not think that this thinking applies here, because the theme of ridding oneself of the privilege of money is a common theme throughout the Bible, and Christ certainly meant it literally when he talked to the rich young man.

Even so, it seems like there is a point in which this thinking can be taken too far. I do think that there is a certain amount of this kind of thinking that is necessary and good for our spiritual development, but if we are constantly thinking about how every dollar we spend could be used to save a life, we will be crushed beneath the weight of the world. As a result, we may become cynical and judgmental, and unable to see the beauty of the world.

The real problem with taking this type of thinking too far is that we may start to think that we can save the world if we try hard enough. We start to think that Jesus *needs us* to fulfill his purpose, and we begin to think that our actions are all too important. We, like Schindler, can be tortured with guilt and shame that we did not do more even when we have done all we can (there is a healthy amount of such guilt, but there is definitely an unhealthy amount as well). The reality is that Jesus doesn't *need* us (individually) in order to accomplish his purposes and to care for the poor. The beauty is that Jesus invites us into his mission of redeeming the world, and I really don't want to miss out on that.

I am convinced that there is a healthy reverence for the thought that every dollar can be used for the benefit of the poor, and there is a healthy amount of pleasure we can enjoy in God's creation. After all, Jesus' first recorded miracle was turning water into wine for a wedding party that had already had their fill of wine! Certainly, God intends us to enjoy this world and many things of this world; for, what could please a creator more than to have others rejoice over their creations?

The real difficulty becomes this: how do we bear the weight of the world while also enjoying the beauty of God's creation? I have the tendency to focus all my effort toward bearing the world's weight, but I also know others whose tendency is to just enjoy the world and its pleasures without a thought of the need in the world. The narrow path is to glory in God's creation and to bear the weight of the world.

Who is my Neighbor?

Jesus emphasizes that when we see injustice, we seek to bring about justice - social justice, economic justice, health justice, all forms of justice, etc. Anywhere someone is oppressed, we seek to "suffer with" (show compassion) them and speak up for those who cannot speak up for themselves. We could get caught up all day in an argument about whether it is okay to own more than another person, but, in reality, that argument will get us nowhere. We are called to be faithful, and, if we are faithful with whatever we have, I am sure that God will be in it. But, the real question behind all the questions posed in this chapter is, "am I being faithful?" As the good Samaritan saw the man bleeding on the side of the road, we too are to stop and mend one another's wounds. Perhaps, the greatest sin a Christian can commit is to pass by their neighbor who needs help. James Keenan defines sin as "the failure to bother to love."[22] We are only asked to be faithful wherever God has placed us - faithful to our neighbors, those whom God has placed around us that are in need. And, *to be faithful* is to bother to love.

In this globalizing society, the definition of neighbor is expanding, for we are now neighbors to many different types of people that we weren't before. And, with technology, almost everyone on earth has the potential to be our neighbor. The neighbor becomes anyone in the world who is in need whom we have means to help. Since this is the case, I believe that the church and all Christians have a greater calling than ever to look within and beyond their borders to meet the needs of this ever-shrinking world. It is overwhelming, but remember - just be faithful, and help whoever you can in whatever situation God has placed you in. And, perhaps, ask Jesus if there are any "neighbors" you haven't yet noticed.

The greatest commandment in the Bible is to "love God and to love neighbor." The Pharisees dwelled on the question, *"who is my neighbor?,"* as an excuse to treat some people as non-neighbors; for, if one can categorize someone as a non-neighbor then one doesn't have to treat them as a neighbor. But, when someone finally asked Jesus, "who is my neighbor?"[23] Jesus responded with a story that implied that the stranger is thy neighbor and that we should not be so concerned with "who is our neighbor" as we should be with *to whom we ought to be neighborly to.*

Gustavo Gutierrez said that my neighbor "is not the one who me I find in my path, but rather he in whose path I place myself, he whom I actively approach and seek."[24] Therefore, any excuse that one has "no needy neighbors" becomes lame and irrelevant. As Jesus walked from village to village to find those who were in need of a neighbor, we too are not to sit comfortably at home and wonder, "where are all the needy neighbors?" They are everywhere, if we would only let Jesus take over our lives and expand our definitions of what a neighbor is.

On a practical note, I think that when we read the news and come across atrocities happening in the world and even our own countries; we are practicing something very dangerous. We read stories of natural disasters, atrocities, racism, sexism, riots, refugee crises, genocide, and the such happening around the world – and we often think, *"how horrible,"* then stop there and say to ourselves, *"there's nothing I can do about it."* Or maybe, at best, we pray a little prayer and go on with our day because we have things to do and money to make. This, in a way, mirrors the story of the good Samaritan. We see people, literally beaten and left for dead on the side of the road, but we tell ourselves that we have more important things to attend to or that it's too bad we don't have the means to help.

One might consider whether watching or reading the news makes one responsible to help those in need. When we read the news, we may respond, "If I was their neighbor I would help them," and then think "too bad I am not their neighbor." Instead, we must ask ourselves, "Is this someone to whom I can be a neighbor to?" When we read the news, it should burden us greatly, for we know we could actually do something about it if we decided to. But, the moment someone says we can do something about it, our defenses go up and we start making excuses. It is no wonder the public and media, at large, ignore the atrocities going on in the developing world while focusing on stories that may be silly or less atrocious local events. I say we better stop reading the news, unless we are looking for places that need people to serve. We better stop paying attention to the news, lest our hearts become cold and we, like the priest on his way to do something religious, become accustomed to ignoring the person bleeding on the side of the road. By being so knowledgeable about the atrocities in the world

and doing nothing about it, it is worth considering that we
might be heaping condemnation upon ourselves.

Assuming God's Will

So far in this book, I feel as if I have been dancing around
being too "heavy hitting" and tried to be gentle. But I feel
that I cannot hold back any longer and I must speak out
against the way the world has slipped into the image of the
church and prevented it from making God known in the
world. Jesus came to open our eyes to the ways in which we
were not reflecting his image. As we have already
established, what he said was quite radical and offensive to
the privileged people in his day. In the same way, Jesus can
be quite radical and offensive − even to the church of this
day. If we really hear Christ's call clearly, it will most likely
make us uncomfortable and squirm in our seats. You may
or may not agree with my "radical" Christianity that I think
should be the norm. If you would forgive me, I am going to
let loose in the next few paragraphs (perhaps, read it in the
voice of a distressed preacher). I only wish that it be read
with humility, openness, and discernment.

We often take Jesus' commands or commissions and act
like obeying them is the exception to the rule as opposed to
the rule. For example, Jesus says to *sell all you have*, and we
respond by saying only a select few should really do that;
He says to *go into all the earth*, and we respond by saying that
mission work is a calling for only a select few. This pattern
repeats itself through our Christianity: Jesus' radical
commands are only to be followed by a radical and foolish
few while the rest of us can live more rational and realistic
lives. Words Christ intended us to hear are words we don't
take seriously. As a result, we tend not to do anything

drastic unless God specifically tells us to do something specific. All the while, we most likely believe God probably won't tell us to do anything specific. Therefore, we are off the hook from living a radical life. But, what if we actually took what Jesus said to do and did it? – sounds simple.

I think that one of the biggest problems (sins) we have in privileged Christianity today is that we automatically *assume* what we are supposed to do (or not do) for Christ; often, by observing what the Christians around us are doing – or even, by observing what the culture around us is doing. One way in which we do this is by seeing how the world lives their lives and adopting the same kind of lifestyle. This, I think most would agree is how a Christian is not supposed to live. The Jesus who came to this earth was rather counter-cultural; yet, it seems that most in the church are being discipled by the norms and values of the culture as opposed to Christ. Lifestyles remain largely undifferentiated from the world at large - the only difference is that it is disguised with evangelical overtones. In this way, we are deceiving ourselves into thinking we are different from the world, yet we are still copying the patterns and behaviors of the world. Yet, Jesus came to free us from the patterns of this world and transform us by the renewal of our minds.[25] He came to alter the way we see the world and, therefore, how we live in the world.

We must stop assuming how we are to live according to the people around us, but instead, according to what we have heard from Jesus. For example, this might mean that we don't follow the pattern of go to school, get a high-paying job, get a spouse, have happy children, retire, and enjoy the last days of life. Jesus should transform us from living according to culture's ideals into pure, orthodox, radical Christianity.

I feel like so many people are afraid to tell you that God has a specific plan and purpose for you, because they don't want to scare you into thinking that you could miss God's will for them. But, even if God *does* have a specific plan and purpose just for you, if you miss a step along the way, God will not abandon you. He can still pick you up and use you just as much as he could have before you messed up. One verse that comes to mind in regard to this is Philippians 2:12: "Work out your salvation with fear and trembling." The problem is that we want to take the fear and trembling out of following God. We are quick to follow God when we feel comfortable and have a certain amount of control. However, biblically, God is *holy*. God is so holy that men would fall down dead if they entered his presence inappropriately. And, this fear and trembling is definitely not just an Old Testament phenomenon. At Jesus' death, the earth quaked, and the veil was torn; surely, these initiated the response of fear and trembling. Therefore, even as salvation was being accomplished and people were granted access to God's presence, there was fear and trembling. Even in Jesus' vulnerable and humiliating death, there was trembling. *Surely this was the Son of God.* Even, when God made himself the very least of all, submitting to even death on a cross, he showed himself to the world and the world trembled. This is how Jesus showed himself to us.

Similarly, when we approach the cross, are we the middle-class Americans, self-sufficient and proud, or are we trembling? For, are we not also those criminals who hung alongside Christ? Are we not the Roman centurion who pierces his side? Are we not those who wept at the cross? Are we not the ones who re-nail him to the cross with every occasion we contribute to the Cycle of Violence? Surely, we are each of those. A certain amount of fear and trembling is to be assumed before him. This is not a fear of punishment but a simple awe and utter devastation which comes when we realize that God has revealed himself to us. Therefore, we fear and tremble that we might do God's will on this earth.

Luckily, God's will is not, for the most part, some mysterious thing that we have to wait around to be gradually revealed to us. It is not something that we have to completely guess what it is for our lives, for he has already miraculously revealed it to us through his word - the Bible. God has already provided "everything we need to live a godly life"[26] through his word and the Holy Spirit. It's as simple as this: If we obey the words of Christ, we will find ourselves in the center of God's will. Therefore, if Jesus says, "care for orphans and widows," do it. If Jesus says, "go into all the world," do it. If Jesus says, "feed the hungry, clothe the naked," do it. I guarantee you that if you put your faith in Jesus' saving acts and do what he commanded, he will not be disappointed in you and say, "You blew it, I had plans for you and you didn't do nothing long enough for me to reveal my will for you." No, he will say, "Well done good and faithful servant."[27]

But if we live our lives doing what *we* desire and sit around waiting for Jesus to tell us what to do, we are in danger of the fires of hell! We are in danger of being the ones who say "Lord, Lord," and he respond, "*Away from me. I never knew you,*[28] *for narrow is the gate that leads to life.*[29]

So many of us fall into the mindset that we must not do anything until God tells/calls us to do it; all the while, God has already told us what to do via his Word. James 1:27 says, "pure and genuine religion is taking care of widows and orphans in their distress and keeping oneself unstained from the world;" Francis Chan responds to this verse by saying, "Why don't we assume adoption as God's will for our lives? and only when we hear a voice from heaven tell us not to, do we stop."[30] We shouldn't be asking, is it God's will for us to adopt? We should be asking, is it God's will for us *not* to adopt? And if we don't hear a distinct "no," we do it. We sit around and wait for Jesus to tell us what to do when he has already told us and exemplified it! We must assume action! And only when we hear a voice from heaven telling us to stop will we stop. Why don't we assume adoption? Why don't we assume missions? Why don't we assume singleness? Why don't we assume giving to the poor? Why don't we assume poverty? We must wrestle with these questions.

Lord, help us to believe what you have said and actually do it. Forgive us for our complete misunderstanding of who you are.

Fruitfulness and Multiplying

The very first commission that humanity received was to "be fruitful and multiply." Many insist that this is the first *command* God made to humanity; but, the Bible does not say that it was a command. Genesis[31] says that "God *blessed* them and said to them, 'be fruitful and multiply. Fill the earth and subdue it. Rule over the fish in the sea and...'" These two blessings can be summarized simply (1) to multiply and (2) to rule. We have already discussed that mankind was created to rule, and now we will discuss the idea that mankind was created to multiply.

Many have taken this passage and interpreted it narrowly to mean that the primary purpose of marriage is to produce offspring. Therefore, if a married couple does not have children, or if someone doesn't get married, then they cannot fulfill one of the key duties of mankind. I think that this is one of the reasons why, throughout history, women have often been reduced to the role of "baby making machines." In such, the value of a woman is found in her ability to produce offspring. This is not just found in secular society but was even deeply embedded into Old Testament stories. Story after story in the Old Testament, women who couldn't get pregnant were looked down upon by the culture around them; not only that, but women without children were also often considered to lack the favor of God. But I am convinced that the blessing to "be fruitful and multiply; fill the earth" was never meant to demean women to this point, nor can it be applied only to women.

Surely, in the Genesis sense, God intended this blessing to entail that they have many children. But I think that this blessing to "be fruitful and multiply" has a much deeper meaning than that. For, if this was meant as a commission to people to produce children, Jesus failed wonderfully at this point.

One of the primary theories for why God created humanity is that *God is love* and *that love is meant to be shared.* And, love, at its core, has this "need" to expand and grow, and create. Therefore, God created humanity to share in this love. Similarly, humanity, being in God's image, has a natural, created tendency to desire love and to expand their love beyond themselves. Therefore, humans desire to have children and form families because of their desire to allow love to expand and multiply. So, when God gives humanity the commission to be fruitful, multiply, and to fill the earth, he is, in a sense, initiating humanity to fill the earth with love and allow it to grow and expand. But the motivation of love is often replaced by other motivations due to the fall of humanity.

When God created humanity, he gave his commission to be fruitful and multiply and fill the earth. But, when God created the *new humanity* with the resurrection of Christ, they received a new commission: "Go, and make disciples of all nations"[32] – *to be fruitful and make disciples.* This reframing of the original commission reveals humanity's call in the context of redemption. Their commission is not to simply produce offspring; their primary commission is to make disciples. Today, it seems that many are stuck in the first commission (still a good thing) when we should be focused on the great commission (the better thing). I often hear parents say that our greatest calling in life is to focus on the blood-related family; all the while, Jesus makes it clear that our calling in life is to seek out the vulnerable who are outside of our genetic circle. In the first commission, our love expanded through the creation of *new human beings*, but now, in the great commission, our love expands through the creation of the *new humanity*. Jesus came to expand our hearts to embrace those outside of who we would normally meet. He came to show us what it really means to be fruitful and multiply: to fill the earth and subdue it.

Jesus reveals God's intention for humanity – that they would be redeemed into his image and that their primary blessing is to help others have access to that redemption. This is what it means to be fruitful. Therefore, the call of Christ is none other than the call to be a disciple-maker, a missionary, and a baptizer. One interesting thing is that our church today likes to emphasize "Go and make disciples" as the call of all disciples – often ignoring the "of all nations" part of the commission. The "of all nations" aspect is reserved for special people who are missionaries or whose focus is cross-cultural ministry. Many missionaries I know is frustrated at this point – don't all Christians realize that the call to make *disciples of every nation* is the call of every Christian? To which, most privileged Christians respond – we need people here to make disciples too, or "there's a lot of need here too." And, I will be the first to admit that there is increasing need in the West; I would also like to note that the West is uniquely situated to reach people of all nations. For, no longer does one need to go overseas to reach people from a country across the world. The world is coming to us. I went to university with people from countries that do not allow Christian missions! What an amazing opportunity that didn't exist even just a hundred years ago.

Even so, the people who are coming to the West are often coming from wealthy families – that is why they can afford to come to a university here. Therefore, using this as an excuse for not needing to send Christians overseas leaves many of "the least of these" in those countries never to be touched by the love of Christ. Surely, we need disciple makers in the West; but surely, those who have never heard the name of Jesus, or have no means of learning about him, need disciple makers all the more. At least people in the West know if they ever feel the need for God, they can go to any church on any city block. But, in some places around the world, even if someone felt the need for God, they have no church in which they could go to find God. Surely, the excuse that we "need workers here" loses all ground on this reality. We who have privilege, authority, and ability, should use our advantage for the advantage of the disadvantaged – and if we are missing the billions of unreached least of these, we need to seriously reconsider where we are placing our resources.

Prayer and Action

Prayer is one of the central, most important, yet also neglected disciplines in the Church. Jesus often went off alone to pray, and the body of Christ is called to do the same. Furthermore, A body that is not driven by prayer is a body that is not being led by the Christ. We must spend time daily with Christ, ensuring we are in line with his Spirit and interceding for the needs of the world. The Bible says Jesus is always interceding for us at the right hand of the Father.[33] And, what Christ is to us, we are to be for the world. So, we are called to be a royal priesthood interceding for the world. For the sins of the world and for the redemption of the world.

We are called to lift prayers for all on earth and that God's kingdom would come. *Seek first his kingdom.*[34] And, an integral part of God's kingdom is righteous justice. We pray for those who are oppressed - that Jesus would be with them in their suffering, that he would hear their cries and deliver them. For refugees from Myanmar, Syria, Central America, South Sudan, and all the other places I am unaware of. For those who suffer genocide, persecution, famine, wars, violence, drugs, sex trafficking, and all the other evils that go on in this world. We pray, and how does God answer those prayers?

Primarily, I think God works through his body. After all, if we ask Jesus to move, what else should we expect to move except his body! And his body is us. Therefore, when we ask Jesus to move, we ourselves are being called to move by Jesus himself. When we ask God to take care of the homeless, we, his body, does so. When we ask God to have compassion on refugees, we go and suffer with them and

love them. When we ask God to save the lost, we go and
share the good news.

After all, *What good is it to say, "Keep warm, be well fed,"
yet do nothing for them?*[35] Faith without action is dead.
Similarly, prayers prayed without the movement of Jesus'
body are dead. Prayer doesn't end when we say "Amen."
Yes, God works miracles that move beyond us as the body;
but, God seems to primarily work through people and use
means which already inhabit this earth. This is perhaps one
of the reasons we often don't explicitly see God's hand in
the Privileged World.

The book of Nehemiah in the Bible provides excellent
examples of prayer inspiring movement. When God's
people pray, God's people are called to move. Nehemiah
hears of the injustice that is happening in and to Jerusalem
(the city of God's temple), and he weeps and prays that God
would bring about justice; then, God sends Nehemiah to be
the leader of the movement to rebuild the walls of the city.[36]
When we see injustice surrounding God's temple (aka the
people of God), we grieve; our hearts break at the
desecration of God's dwelling, and we cry out to God. And,
when we pray for the injustice in the world, we are, in a way,
also asking God to send us to work against that injustice.
Repeatedly, in the book of *Nehemiah*, action always follows
prayer. Another instance in *Nehemiah* is when the Israelites
prayed for God's protection, and then went on to post
guards to protect the builders.[37] They weren't showing
their disbelief that God could protect them by posting
guards; they were simply acting as those who knew a God
who primarily works through his people. It's as if they
followed the principle: Pray as if everything depends on
God, and act as if everything depends on you. Then, when

you are successful, give all glory to God and take no credit of your own.

We often like to pray that God would send someone else, but often when we pray, we often are, ourselves, the means through which God wants to use to bring about his will. The very feeling of being prompted to pray for someone or something may be the first sign that the Holy Spirit is prompting you to work to bring a godly presence into that specific situation. Prayer is always to be coupled with action; for, *faith without works is dead.*[38] In praying, we show faith; in action, our faith comes to completion. Sending "prayer and blessing" to those who need help without helping them runs the risk of being an insincere prayer. The words, "I'll pray for you," become words that help ease our conscience and trick our minds into thinking that we are doing the "Christian thing" without having to personally become involved in another individual's situation – it is a spiritualized unwillingness to not bear one another's burdens. James even says, "Can such faith save them? Suppose a brother or a sister is without clothes and daily food. If one of you says, 'Go in peace; keep warm and well fed,' but does nothing about their physical needs, what good is it? In the same way, faith by itself, if it is not accompanied by action is, dead."[39]

In the same way, when we pray for the needs of others, but do nothing to help them, we are making a mockery out of faith. Therefore, when we pray for the needs of the persecuted church, for refugees, for the imprisoned, the hungry, the poor, and the needy, but do nothing for their physical well-being we are praying faithless prayers. Pope Francis says it simply, "You pray for the hungry, then you feed them. That is how prayer works."

Certainly, there are times in which all we can do is pray and there is nothing we can do to help. In some situations, the only way to partake in the bearing of another's burden is to *pray*. Even so, there are a multitude of times we pray for something that God is indeed calling his Body to act for. We pray for justice, and we are called to work for justice. Justice is what prayer looks like in public.[40]

It is not that God needs people in order to accomplish his will, but that he chooses to use people. And, God, by all means, does not need *you or me* in order to accomplish his will. God can save the world without you. But God gives us this grand privilege of being able to be his body to the world and to be Christ to the world. He found it fitting to involve humans in the redemption of this world. Humans, who colluded with Satan and messed up the world in the first place, are given a second chance and become a part of the story for creation's redemption. In great patience, Jesus treats us with much dignity by including us in his plans to redeem the world. Therefore, let us join in the work with joy and know that, if we accomplish anything, it is not by our power and might, but through Jesus and his Spirit. *Praise God that we get the privilege of being involved in his work.*

5

HUMANITY IN PERSPECTIVE

> Make sure no outsider who follows God ever has occasion
> to say, "God put me in second-class. I don't really belong."
> And make sure no physically mutilated person is ever
> made to think, "I'm damaged goods. I don't really belong."
> For God says: "…I'll provide them an honored place in my
> family and within my city, even more honored than that of
> sons and daughters. I'll confer honors on them that will
> never be revoked."
>
> - Isaiah 56:3;5 MSG

An Other-Focused Perspective

In the last couple chapters, we focused on the characteristics
of Christlikeness (humility and authority), the actions that
take place because of those characteristics (leveraging and
laying down), and the global extent to which those actions
are to be implemented. However, these characteristics and
actions do not appear out of thin air; Christ must transform
us into his image and, in doing so, completely reshape our
perspectives. We must be given the eyes of Christ that we
might practice these characteristics and actions out of a
genuine heart – not out of mere effort or legalism. Ideally,
we do not risk all for Christ because we feel he demands it
from us; but because we *want* to risk all for Christ. We

become the *type of person* who willingly lays down their life for our friends; not as one who lays down their life out of a compulsion to obey the letter of the law. The brutality of the cross and life of the Christian are mere side-effects of the transformation of the heart and mind into the image of Christ. If the actions of laying down and leveraging become the end goal of faith, then it becomes an empty and legalistic gospel. These actions are to come out of a transformed heart that changes how we see and interact with the world. We can lay down and leverage everything, but if our hearts are not transformed, it is all meaningless. As in the example of the widow's penny, it is the heart that Christ really cares about.

Christ transforms the Christian into his image, and in this, their eyes are enabled to see others as God sees them; they are more able to recognize the image of God in others. Only in as much as we see with the eyes of Jesus are we Christlike. Christ is the head of the body; therefore, he is also to be our mind and our eyes. If we are to truly understand this world, it will come through a godly vision of the world.

Christ should change how we, as individuals and as the body, see others. Without Christ working through us, it would be ridiculous to say that we are to be *Christ to the world*. But, since we are his body, we must humbly accept that we are Christ to the world in some manner or other. Only when we realize that we could never be Christ on our own do we become a body part that God can use. He must become more; we must become less.[1] We must focus less on how *we* can make *ourselves* more like Christ and begin to focus on the *other*. Being Christlike means that we become otherly-focused. First, it means focused on the other who is

God; then, naturally, focused on the other who is our neighbor.

I think we, especially as humans living in an individualized culture, tend to place ourselves as the main focus in life. Even our Christian walk may be focused much on our own personal development. But, as we become more Christlike, this focus is to shift outward - so much so that the self is lost in its service of others and captured by the beauty of the image of God in others. No longer do we become so obsessed with our own Christlikeness and spiritual development, but instead, we see the hidden beauty in others as God's most precious creation. We might even become obsessed with other people in a certain sense - that we just notice the godlike in others and cannot help but rejoice and find joy in others. It is when we stop focusing on and looking at ourselves, that we can begin to see God. And, a true vision of God always has the impact of making one like him; therefore, once we have a vision of who God is, then we will be able to see humanity as God intends us to see.

The Perspective of Jesus

Something happens when we look at Christ, we inevitably become more like him and our vision starts to be transformed.[2] When we look into the eyes of the one who represents humanity, we begin to see humanity as God intended. Since we see through the eyes of *the son of humanity*, everyone becomes our brothers and sisters. *This is the heart and soul of the Christian message: that humans are precious and sacred in the sight of God.* If we could just understand this one concept, then the whole story of the Bible begins to make sense; and the whole meaning of life

falls into place. Jesus cares deeply about the human
condition. That is why Jesus has a special place in his heart
for the poor and the marginalized – he sees *his precious
humanity* being neglected. This is the most atrocious thing
in Christ's eyes. This is why God rages in the Old
Testament over injustice. This is why Jesus rages in the
temple – making a whip (the only time we know that Jesus
held a weapon), flipping over tables, and throwing money
on the ground - when he sees people exploiting the
vulnerable in the very place where God and humanity are
supposed to be revered.[3]

Injustice, poverty, sickness, starvation, and oppression
are all things God hates. These are the results of evil and
are all things that cast disrespect on the image of God. Just
as God rages at those who perpetrate injustice and those
who stand idly by, Jesus has a soft spot in his heart for the
poor and needy. The Great Physician has more compassion
and patience for the sick than he has for the healthy. It
might seem unfair to us that God would favor the poor; but
injustice has given him no choice. He looks on them with
compassion and sadness, that his most precious creation
would be allowed to live in such conditions.

I often think of the parable of the woman washing Jesus'
feet with perfume. The disciples scoff at how she is wasting
something that could have been given to the poor. Jesus
replies, *you will always have the poor among you, but my body
will not always be here.*[4] In saying so, Jesus implies that it is
true that it is good sell our valuables and give to the poor
just as the woman took her valuables and lavished them on
Christ. What's even more significant is that Jesus is still
here among us in the body of the poor. Jesus is the least of
these, and whatever we do unto them we are doing unto
him. Just as the place of worship was transferred from the

temple to the body of Christ - the new place of worship has been transferred from Christ to the body of the poor! Every human being, simply on this account, is worthy of deep respect and reverence. When we start seeing things from Jesus' perspective, everything changes. The human condition is one that is sacred to God and thus, should be to us. Any insult on humanity becomes an insult on God; therefore, justice should be dear to the heart of every Christian.

John the Baptist (the man Jesus said was the greatest among the living![5]) says that he is not even worthy to untie the straps of Jesus' sandals - a task only done by a servant. In doing so, he says that he is not worthy of even serving Christ, or of being his servant.[6] Yet, Jesus himself calls us to be his servant - giving us the privilege and making us worthy. If we are not even worthy of serving Christ, then we are all the more unworthy of Christ being our servant! Yet, Christ himself washed the disciple's feet. He came not to be served, but to serve.[7] Those not worthy of being Christ's servant are now being served by Christ! As Christ has served us, we are to serve the world.

Jesus said, w*hatever you do unto the least of these, you do unto me.*[8] When we serve others, we are really serving Christ. From a worldly point of view, serving Christ is not glamorous, for *he had no beauty or majesty to attract us to him, nothing in his appearance that we should desire him. He was despised and rejected by mankind, a man of suffering, familiar with pain. He was an eyesore and we held him in low esteem.*[9] Yet, it is this Jesus we serve when we serve the poor. When we wash the homeless man's feet, we are washing the feet of Christ. When we take off their stenching dirty socks, we are untying Christ's sandals. This is something we are not even worthy to partake in! When we serve the poor, keeping this in mind will help one understand what a great privilege it is. When we are bandaging the rotting foot, we are doing something of great privilege of which we are completely unworthy of doing. Yet, Christ has made us worthy and, therefore, we rejoice in the honor of serving Christ in the world. The humble dirty task of a servant becomes the task given to a servant of high regard.

   "We find the Lord in our encounters with man, especially the poor, marginalized, and exploited ones. An act of love toward them is an act of love towards God." – Gustavo Gutierrez[10]

Seeing Christ Everywhere

As we gaze upon Jesus something happens, and we start to see Jesus everywhere; for we begin gazing into the eyes of the least of these. We gaze into Jesus' eyes and we find ourselves looking into the eyes of the beggar, the homeless, our neighbors, our friends, and everyone we meet. The Christian sees Christ everywhere. But to make it clear, this gaze must start on Jesus; for, if we begin by looking for the divine within others without first looking at Christ, we may become confused and miss Jesus completely. We must spend time in intimate communion with Christ in order to know what he looks like – we must be connected to the head. What does this even mean?

   We keep connected to the head through constant communion with him in prayer. Prayer must become a way of life. Since prayer and action are intimately intertwined; Sometimes our prayers may be prayed by our actions and service. Or other times it is wordless groans. Overall, prayer is the lifestyle of interaction with Christ; *it is the communication of one's spirit with God's Spirit.* Prayer is the meditation of one's heart that is submitted to God.

Bible reading and private prayer are extremely important disciplines, but sometimes we stop there and don't move on into equally important spiritual disciplines. Since we encounter the Lord in our encounters with man, I am convinced that spending time in community is one of the primary ways we spend time with Jesus. The way we treat others when we spend time with others, can also be a form of prayer. We communicate much to God in the way we treat other humans. We can either be singing his praises or blaspheming his name in the way we treat others. Our prayer communicates worship when we lift him high; therefore, in our lifting of others, we are communicating worship to God.

It is no wonder that Jesus said the greatest command was to "'Love the Lord your God with all your heart and with all your soul and with all your mind... And the second is *like* it: 'Love your neighbor as yourself.'" [11] Jesus says the second command *is similar to loving God* – almost the same thing. In fact, our primary way of loving God is to love our fellow humans! It is no wonder then, that the fruit of the Spirit is "Love, Joy, Peace, Patience, Kindness, Goodness, Faithfulness, Gentleness, and Self-Control;" [12] for, each of these attributes are put into practice in the context of relationship. The fruit of the Spirit is an increased ability to treat our fellow human beings as God intends for images of God to be treated. Jesus surely treated his neighbor as himself. Jesus was the only perfect image of God, and he surely treated every person as if they were perfect images of God – even though they were filthy with sin.

Humanity as the New Temple

A theme that repeats itself throughout certain psychological disciplines, Eastern religions, and most of those who have tried to discover the meaning in life is that there is a certain sense of connectedness, oneness, or wholeness found in life and in the universe. There also seems to be agreement on a connectedness which one can experience with the universe and others which makes life worth living. This theme inevitably reveals a certain emptiness/incompleteness that exists within the state of the human race that humanity has yet to discover.

In India (the heartland of Hinduism, Buddhism, and Jainism), it is customary to put one's hands together as if they are praying and greet another with the word *namaste*. *Namaste* basically means, "I acknowledge the divine in you." By making this the common greeting, everyone is supposed to be reminded that there is something special and, even, divine about life. There is something profound in putting one's hands together, looking someone in the eye, and saying *namaste* - "I see the divine in you." Furthermore, if one is a guest to a Hindu household, they may put a dot on your forehead and a flower necklace on your neck as a blessing which communicates, "I worship you."

On a visit to India, my host put a necklace around my neck and said, "This means I worship you" and then he laughed and laughed. When every man is a bearer of God's image, every man is in danger (although somewhat amusingly) of mistaking the image of God for God himself. It is no wonder many have noticed the godlike within themself and considered humanity divine (as many Hindus have). On the other hand, when every man is an imperfect image of God, it comes to no surprise that others would say there is nothing special about the human race and that men are nothing more than highly developed animals. Which, ironically, is how many lower-class people in India are treated. The way Hindus are taught to recognize the divine in others, even outside the influence of Christendom's doctrine of the image of God, reveals that there seems to be something in humanity intrinsically recognized as coming from God. But, the way many in India have been dehumanized shows how easy it is for humanity to disregard the divine in man out of convenience.* It is striking to consider how the Hindu doctrine of the "divinity of humanity" parallels the Christian doctrine of "the image of God." In a Christian view, humanity is not worthy of worship because it is not God and is often a sad excuse for an image of God at that.

Even so, Christ has redeemed the human condition and we are invited to enter into the wholeness, connectedness, and oneness of life that is found within Jesus - a oneness birthed out of restored relationships. In Christ's economy of love, love comes full circle.

In the days of old, people had to go to the temple in order to worship. The temple was the one place where God and man could meet. The holy place where heaven and earth overlapped. In our culture, we often misunderstand how significant the concept of the temple really is. We don't understand the reverence or awe the temple entails. In many places around the world, the temple is seen as a *holy* place; a place you must take off your shoes before entering because it is holy ground; a place you must cover your head in humility; a place you face toward when you pray and kiss the ground before entering. Some even make pilgrimages

---

* Although I am speaking of India as an example, I wish to point out that every country and culture seems to have their own ways of and reasons for dehumanizing others.

across the earth to see certain temples. A place where just catching a glimpse of it puts one in closer proximity to God. In Jesus' day, the temple in Jerusalem was this very place - the holiest place on earth. But, Jesus "redefined where God dwelled" and made it a person.[13] And when Christ died, the inch-thick curtain that separated the presence of God from the people in Jerusalem's temple was torn in two as a proclamation that God's presence no longer dwelt in the temple, but in the body of Christ. The body of Christ is now the place of worship.

Now, we live in the age where, through the outpouring of the Holy Spirit, Christ's followers become the very temple that houses the living God.[14] Heaven and Earth meet inside his followers. (This is really a profound miracle that we should meditate much more on.) In fact, *true worshippers' worship in Spirit and in truth & these are the worshippers God seeks. Worship doesn't occur in Jerusalem or on a mountain. Worship occurs in Spirit and in truth.*[15] In this new reality, the Spirit-filled human being now becomes the place of worship! A Spirit-filled humanity is now the temple. We are the temple of the Holy Spirit, bringing the blessing of God's presence to the world. This is a grand mystery that changes the way we see humanity.

When we sing with the Psalmist, "how lovely is your dwelling place"[16] we can also sing, "how lovely is the human that God has chosen to dwell in!" How can this be? How can I be worthy of this? The place of worship is no longer a place one must go, but it is any place where humans gather in God's name. "For, where two or three gather in my name, there am I with them."[17]

If humanity is now the place of worship, the act of worship becomes Christlike love expressed through the service of others. We no longer neglect people for the sake of the temple because now people are the temple. People of all kinds now form the house where God's glory dwells. *My house will be called a house of prayer for all nations.*[18] Jesus further defines the temple as a place that serves the outcasts of society. Jesus admonishes each of us to see *himself* in the people we serve. Particularly, Jesus identifies with the downtrodden and lowly. "Truly I tell you, whatever you did for one of the least of these brothers and sisters of mine, you did for me."[19] Jesus was the son of humanity; therefore, all are his brothers and sisters. That is why Jesus so values humanity and when he sees certain people oppressed and suffering, he sees them and cares for them deeply, longing for us to see people the same way he does. We too are to identify with those who objectively need help, regardless of their religious affiliations. We are not to distinguish between those who are Christian and non-Christians or between temples and non-temples; such thinking only leads to phariseeism and, what's more is that Christ does not make such distinctions in the people he serves – he simply serves all who come to him. Keith Green says that when we love someone in his name, we are loving him.[20] Love of neighbor becomes an expression of our love for God. The human becomes the ultimate place of worship.

The Interconnectedness of Christlike Love

Just by being human, there seems to be a deep level as to which we are connected to the rest of humanity – particularly in attaching ourselves to the son of humanity, we attach ourselves to humanity as a whole. We are the body of Christ called to love Christ in the flesh. Truly, when we love another, we are also loving ourselves. On a deep level, when we love one another as ourselves, we see it as if we are loving ourselves; just as Jesus sees himself in those he serves. We become totally lost in our love for others. The image of God is present in every single human being; therefore, there is no excuse for mistreatment or discrimination and every person is worthy of love and respect. This means refusing to dehumanize anyone and humanizing others even when it doesn't seem they deserve to be treated with such respect.

Jesus takes the idea of the image of God and elevates it to a new level in calling us to identify Jesus with the people that we serve. A deeper understanding of God's image in the world produces in us eyes that love across boundaries that were once thought impossible. We may find ourselves looking with love upon people we once found unable to identify with or even those we once found repulsive. When we consider every man to be a bearer of God's image, then everyone is much more valuable than we can imagine. When we look at our brother, we not only see our brother, but we may be catching a glimpse of God. When we look at the poor and needy, we are looking at Christ himself. A Christian sees God everywhere, and, he is bringing God wherever he goes. In this perspective, life is saturated with the sacred and the holy.

This "seeing Jesus everywhere" is in contrast to the many Christians who only see the devil everywhere - perhaps more common than the former. Many Christians suffer from a paranoia that the devil is out to get them (he certainly is); but in doing so, they forget that Christ in them has all authority on earth. We have nothing to fear if we have Christ living inside of us. A Christian is not to primarily notice the work of the devil in the world. Many obsessed with spiritual warfare think of the devil's working a whole lot more than God's working. A Christian should know the power of God and trust that he is bringing everything to redemption. We are motivated out of God's love and not fear of the evil one.

The Already Present but Not Yet Arrived Kingdom

With all this talk about *seeing* Jesus in the world and *being* Jesus in the world, we must not dive into a sort of "pantheism" where we confuse everything for God. When we talk of such things, we must be grounded in the truth of Christ and not allow this seeing of Jesus everywhere to become everything; lest we run the risk of calling everything sacred, and therefore, nothing being treated as sacred. In such a view, the universe is God, and the ultimate goal is to be absorbed into the oneness of the universe. In this, we run the risk of confusing lightness, with darkness. Further, I am not equating man with God, or necessarily equating man with Jesus in the sense that we are to lift humanity up in worship. We are to be grounded solidly in the truth that we are separate from Jesus and God; but also acknowledge that God has allowed for a deep connection to occur between him, creation, and humankind. And, in seeing this deep connection and cultivating it, we can get a greater revelation of who God is and how he is working. Yet, we are not supposed to be completely satisfied in the way things are in this present age. This satisfaction is one that will only be met when God makes his home on earth and the new kingdom arrives in its fullness. Currently, we can be satisfied in the reality that we *will be* satisfied.

Opposite of pantheism, humans have also tended to have a view of life called "dualism." In dualism, life and creation is seen to be completely godless and evil – having nothing to do with God. This has seeped into Christianity in many regards. For example, Christians can often feel the expectation to become "more spiritual" by rejecting the human and physical aspects of life. Furthermore, creation is often framed as "evil" and God as standing as opposed to the evil creation. In this view, people wait for God to come and destroy creation so that evil will be destroyed with it. It is true that there are evil forces in this world, but those evil forces do not find their origin or eternal home in creation. In a more Christian perspective, creation is subjected to frustration due to the prevalent evil in the world, and things probably will get worse before they get better. But, we cannot let this get in the way of the hope we have that creation will be liberated from bondage and decay.[21]

Both pantheism and dualism result from worldviews that contend with a Biblical worldview. God created the world, and "it was good." Yes, it was corrupted, but that does not make it beyond redemption. The image of God is what humanity is made in, and the Christian life is one that returns humanity to the place God intends for them to be. The Christian doesn't become less human, but more human than he or she could ever be on his own; for we are restored back to God's intended image for humanity. We were created to be human on this very earth for a reason. And, Christ's coming to the world in physical form affirms God's value of physical creation. Certainly, the physical is not evil if Christ himself became a physical man who partook in all physical aspects of life. He affirms physicality in that regard;

thus, we follow in his footsteps by being lifted to his level. We are to be people on this earth, with our feet firmly planted on earth. Dietrich Bonhoeffer once wrote, "I fear that Christians who venture to stand on earth on only one leg will stand in heaven on only one leg too."[22] Jesus was obviously committed to the redemption of this earth, and we, just like Jesus must be people committed to the redemption of this earth – not people sitting around waiting for God to destroy it all and remake it. Like Jesus, our feet must be firmly planted on this earth, while also being firmly planted in the kingdom of heaven at the same time. For in Jesus, the kingdom begins to overlap with our present physical reality.

One might wonder how this is possible, but Christ himself said that "the kingdom of heaven is in your midst" – *it has arrived*.[23] Even so, this does not take away from the hope of a future kingdom that has a greater degree of glory. It will be such that the current form of this planet will pass away, and the unseen new creation will appear in greatness.

In considering the resurrection, Christ himself was physically resurrected, but his body was transformed in some manner or another. Thus, when Christ was resurrected, his resurrected body was more real, more perfect than the old. In a sense, he was more physical than ever and yet more full of the breath of God than ever. His physicality surpassed the physicality in this world. In the same sense, we too will be resurrected just as Christ himself was resurrected. We will have physical bodies, but they will be new and will be more human than they ever have been.[24] "For we know that when this earthly tent we live in is taken down we will have a house in heaven, an eternal body made for us by God himself and not by human hands."[25] We will no longer wander in the wilderness with a tent for a temple (as the Israelites did), but we will enter the promise land in the presence of an everlasting temple (as the Israelites hoped their temple would be).

C.S. Lewis talks about this time when the kingdom comes in all its glory as a place that will be more real and more physical than this. So much so that life before this might seem like a passing dream.[26] Our earthy dwelling is like a tent in comparison to the mansion that will be our bodies in heaven. *What is mortal will be swallowed up by life,*[27] and reality will be more real than it has ever been. For a dream may feel real in the moment, but when we wake up, the dream wanes in significance. So, may it be with our lives. Reality as we know it is an illusion in the light of God's kingdom. Jon Walker says, that "as long as we claim [this life] as reality, we will find it difficult to move into the kingdom of heaven."[28] Now, God is making everything good again. Despite evil's desire to keep its grip on creation, our perspective becomes less about evil creation and a good God, but more about a dead creation and a God that breathes his Spirit into creation to make it dance again.

Yet, this view of God reigning does not necessarily paint a rosy picture of the current world; we see the violence and destruction that still persists in this world. There are evil forces we must acknowledge and, as Christians, take head on. "Our struggle is not against flesh and blood" (aka, our struggle is not against physical creation), but "against the rulers, against the authorities, against the powers of this dark world, and against the spiritual forces of evil in the heavenly realms."[29] We confront such evil because there is no place in God's kingdom where violence should abound, and justice be ignored. As we take on the perspective of Jesus where every human is infinitely precious and any injustice against man is an injustice against God; our struggle for the kingdom becomes all the more real and meaningful.

Justice as Addressing Sin

From this 'Jesus point of view,' "Misery and social injustice reveal 'a sinful situation,' a disintegration of brotherhood and communion; by freeing us from sin, Jesus attacks the roots of an unjust order. For Jesus, the liberation of the Jewish people was only one aspect of a universal permanent revolution. Far from showing no interest [in the liberation of the Jewish people from Rome], Jesus rather places it on a deeper level with far reaching consequences."[30] In other words, sin is the reason for poverty and hunger; therefore, by addressing the sin of mankind to fail to love our neighbor, Jesus paves the way for systemic change that brings about his kingdom. In Jesus' kingdom, *every person is precious, and no one is, therefore, deserving of any special privileges over another.* In this new kingdom, there is an end to the domination of man over man; it is a kingdom that contradicts what this world considers a kingdom to be.[31]

Our love for Christ is intimately wound up in our love for others. And since Jesus especially favored the lowly; we, too, who have much, should especially favor the lowly. Justice is the act of working on behalf of the lowly, exploited, and vulnerable. Some have said that "to know God is to do justice."[32] Justice, not done out of a heart of religious obligation, but out of a heart which melts when one sees their fellow man in need. This is the heart Jesus came to give us; and, this is the heart that will bring about his kingdom.

*As Jesus went around to different towns and villages, he
taught in the religious places, proclaimed the arrival of the
kingdom, and healed every kind of disease and sickness.
When he was out and saw the crowds, he had compassion
on them; they were like sheep without a good shepherd –
helpless, harassed, and hurting. Jesus then turned to his
disciples, "look, there is so much to be done, but so very few
people are doing anything. The harvest is ripe. Ask the
Lord of the harvest to send more workers into the harvest
field."* (Matthew 9:35-38, paraphrase).

6

AN EMBRACE OF COMMUNITY

Communion with the Lord inescapably means a Christian life centered around a concrete and creative commitment of service to others.

Gustavo Gutierrez[1]

A School for Christlikeness

Considering how God's values are often so completely different from our own and how rampantly imperfect humans are, it seems that all Christian should be enrolled in a course that systematically teaches us how to be Christlike. Perhaps, assignments could include spending a day with the homeless or giving away one's precious possessions. A pop quiz might include the person you have the most difficulty getting along with coming in for a surprise visit and slapping you in the face to see if you would turn your cheek. No doubt, such a course would probably help us become more Christlike (and I would love to enroll); but, the reality is that Christ has already given us those assignments, and he has already given us a community of peers in which to practice them. We shouldn't need a course to get us to start taking this seriously; for, participation in the church community and life itself is already supposed to be a breeding ground for Christlikeness.

Community* is so central to the Christian faith that a Christian who rejects community could hardly be considered a Christian at all; for, communion between individuals is the natural result of Christlike love. When we are born into Christ, we are born into a new community based on the love of Christ. We become a part of the body of Christ and work to bring his love into all corners of the world. Community is the sign of Christ's love and is to be the place on earth where injustice is met with steadfast grace. It is the place where the kingdom of heaven touches down. If sin is the failure to love, then Christlike community is to be the place where love abounds. The Christlike community is the place where the Cycle of Violence is broken through Christlike bearing of sin and is replaced by a cycle of proactive love and nonviolent resistance.

The Trinity as the Foundational Relationship

It is evident that one of the most basic needs of the human being is to be in relationship with other human beings. God affirmed this when he said that "it is not good for man to be alone."[2] So, by our very nature, it seems that we are made to be in relationship. God did not create man (singular) in the image of God; no, "in the image of God he created *them*" (plural).[3] In saying "them," it is indicated that humans,

---

Community: the phenomenon of "common unity" amidst diverse people living intimately intertwined lives. Common unity ideally results in an environment of support (spiritually and materially), encouragement, accountability, and growth all working toward a common goal or endpoint.

together, are made in God's image – not a single human
alone. It is only in community that man can reflect God's
image. Whether that be the community of marriage or the
community of the church, community is a prerequisite to
bearing God's image. No human, alone, has ever born the
image of God. Even Christ himself did not bear the image
alone, for he existed in perfect union with the Father and
the Holy Spirit.

The Trinity sets a precedent as to how we are made in
the image of God, for God himself exists in the relationship
of the Trinity. In creating humans, God said to himself, "Let
us make mankind in *our* image."[4] First, why would God be
talking to himself? And who is this *us* and *our?* Is not God
one? It is in such passages that we begin to discover the
grand mystery of the Triune God. The oneness and the
triunity that exists in God exists beyond our current
categories and vocabulary in a way that makes it impossible
to comprehend or understand completely. Yet, within the
incomprehensible Trinity we discover a glimpse of God's
plan for how humans are to live and gain insight into the
human condition as God created it. Within God himself,
there is a community: The Father, the Son, and the Holy
Spirit; it is only in community that God exists; therefore, it
is only in relationship/community that mankind can reflect
God's image. Furthermore, the community of Christ
reflects God's image more fully than the sum of each
individual image bearer. It is truly when the church the
community of the love of Christ that the world truly sees
the physical image of the invisible God. I cannot stress
enough the important role of Christian community in the
transformation of the believer and in revealing Christ's
image to the world. It is essential.

On a deeper level, Jesus himself alludes to the idea that
the Trinity is to be a model for Christian love and life.
Oneness was Christ's prayer for the church. *That they may
be one, just as the Father and I are one.*[5] When the reality of
this sinks in, the improbability and impossibility of this also
sets in. How can we as believers on earth be one, as God the
Trinity is one? *God is one.* The Father, The Son, The Holy
Spirit: each different, yet in such perfect unity that they are
one. Each equally the one God. The Trinity is the perfect
manifestation of diversity within unity. Each member is
distinct - they must communicate with one another (i.e.,
Jesus prayed to the Father). The Trinity, God, is a
relationship within and of himself. Each is in perfect
harmony with the other and in perfect relationship with one
another. Such oneness is impossible for such humans living
in a world where all that is known is broken relationships.

God is love, and love is not love unless it is shared; and,
God was love before he created us. Since God is the Trinity,
love has been shared within himself from all eternity. God
has always been love. For all eternity, God has been the
perfect model for how relationships should be. The Trinity
is always worshipping and praising one another, constantly
submitting to one another in love - *not my will, but Thy will.*
Love is the binding component of the Trinity. God is one,
because God is love.

In the same way, *the two shall become one* in love in
marriage.[6] It was in this essence that man was made in the
image of God. God is love, and we are made in his image;
this means that we were created for love, for relationship.
We do not reflect God's image unless we are in loving
relationship with others. This has explicit implications for
all relationships: our marriages and our friendships. It is
this divine love that allows for the miracle of oneness among

those who know him. It is this divine love that binds his creation as one. This love creates oneness amidst diversity. We become absorbed into one another in a way; we become all about the interests of others and are constantly adoring, serving, and loving one another.

Broken Relationships made Whole

Since the very beginning, humanity was made to reflect God's image through a oneness expressed in loving relationships. However, this love was ruined at the fall and, therefore, the part of man that reflects God's image was darkened. When Adam ate the fruit, relationships were broken and as a result, the image of God was darkened in man. Humanity was no longer able to live in perfect relationship with God, no longer able to live in perfect relationship with other humans, and no longer able to live in perfect relationship to creation. Nevertheless, humanity still reflects God's image in some manner by the fact that we must still live in relationship - albeit, broken relationships. This state of broken relationships is responsible for everything that has gone wrong in the world. Dean Sherman says that "every problem is a relationship problem"[7] – surely, this is self-evidently true. Jesus came to redeem these relationships that we might once again live according to God's image. That is the gospel in a nutshell.

If broken relationships are what Jesus came to redeem, it is no surprise that God's plan for the redemption of these relationships would primarily involve establishing a relational community centered on Christ (the perfect image). For, in a community of Christlike relationships, the image of God is restored. The word, *Church* has been used in so many ways that we can find it easy to forget what it even means anymore. At the heart of it, the church is simply a group of Christians that gather together; but, we often forget that the purpose of the church is to gather, in relationship, in community, with other individuals for the magnification of Christ's image in the world. It is within this community that the image of God is supposed to be restored. The church is to be a place of restored relationships - between God and man, between man and man, and between creation and man - and as a result of these restored relationships, Christ is shown to the world. I believe that such a church is the type of church to which God has called us. A church where we go to be in relationship - not a place to sing songs, listen to a nice speaker, be filled with nice thoughts, be entertained, make connections so we don't feel lonely, but a place of intimate relationships that are messy and beautiful. Such an environment makes complete sense for what God wants to do.

It is easy to look at the idea of "community" and eagerly desire to be a part of something so beautiful. But we should be fair warned; Christian community is not something that is birthed easily but will naturally come with as much blood, sweat, and tears that were shed on the path to the cross. It will put to the test every aspect of the Christian faith and will even push some to leave the faith entirely. It is to be training ground for Christlikeness. It is beautiful in that it is a place of restored relationships and it is brutal in that it is a place of restored relationships; for restored relationships don't just happen at the snap of the fingers. To cultivate such community, we will need to practice the same humility and authority that we discussed in Chapter 3. Embracing of others requires a laying down of oneself for the sake of others; it is the death of oneself. But, in dying to ourselves and embracing life together as God's calling on our lives, we all may be resurrected together as one body – the living body of Christ.

We die to ourselves, but we do not consider it a death to one's individuality; but an expansion of one's individuality to take on the identity of Christ. We were once dead, but now, in Christ, we are truly what we were created to be.

Laying Down Cultural Privilege

Bringing this discussion back to the context of privilege, it seems that we have much to learn when it comes to embracing Christlike community. One area for improvement that particularly stands out to me is our embrace of those who are different from us in any way. I first started wrestling with these ideas when one of my close friends mentioned it to me while we were sitting in the campus coffee shop at our university.

My friend is ethnically Hmong - a ethnic group hailing from South and East Asia. I had never really considered his race as that big of a deal, and I assumed that it didn't really influence much of his life - this shows how easy it is to be ignorant of our own privilege and of other people's lack of privilege. In truth, I should emphasize that *we often don't realize that we are privileged until we come face to face with those who have less privilege than us.* I was surprised and heartbroken when he started explaining to me that he struggled much with his identity as a Hmong and his relationship to White Christians. He told me that he wished he was White so that when he went to church or Christian events, people wouldn't treat him differently. In later conversations he confessed a deep anger at White Christians for their ignorance to their own biases.

As a White Christian, I was appalled at my fellow believers for their shallow view and understanding of race and ethnicity - and perhaps afraid that I myself, as a White Christian, had contributed to this ignorance. In the moments afterward, I realized how ignorant and shallow our understanding of culture, ethnicity, and race is as the privileged church. In addressing this issue, Martin Luther King Jr. wrote that "Whites...are not putting in a mass effort to re-educate themselves out of their racial ignorance.... It is an aspect of their sense of superiority that the White people of America believe they have so little to learn."[8] Although this was written during the civil rights era, I believe it stands true for today.

I apologized to my friend on behalf of White people and myself for making him wish that he were White so we wouldn't treat him differently. Yet, an apology is not enough. A simple apology can lead to what psychologists call "moral licensing." An example of this is when someone has one Black friend and, because of this, assumes that they are not racist even though they continue to hold racist views and prejudices (i.e., a politician who brings their Latino friend on stage to prove they're not racist and then goes on to develop policies that exclude and harm that very people group). By having "token" friends, we may be deceiving ourselves into thinking we have no bias. In the same way, this ignorance can continue when one thinks they have done a good thing by apologizing and think they can move on without needing to change anything (i.e., apologizing to Native Americans for taking their homes and destroying culture and then saying, "can't they get over what happened years ago?"). We must be careful that we don't stop at apologizing and use our apology as an excuse to never change our actual behavior. We must strive for a deeper understanding that will transform our relationships and push us into the God-intended life that flows from those relationships.

If our treatment of my friend causes him to wish his skin were a different color, we are in the wrong. My friend, made in the image of God, should not wish he were a different color. To cause someone to feel that the image of God that they were made in is an absolute disgrace and is a great sin.

In awareness of these complexities, some have cultivated a strict "colorblind" denial of diversity by denying any differences of skin tone or culture. I do not think this is the answer to such difficulties, for God must have created different colors of human beings because one color would not do justice to the magnificence of God. God created many cultures, because one culture would not do justice to the massiveness of God nor to the beauty of humanity.

The color of skin should not be ignored but celebrated with an understanding that it is only a superficial difference. There is much more to a person than their skin - there is their culture, their history, their experiences - all things that cannot be determined by the color of one's skin. Each man is unique. We should praise God when we get to worship alongside another whose skin and culture is different than ours, for Christ is magnified and we enter into a celebrated biblical vision of worship - where every tongue and nation is praising God; indeed, we catch a glimpse of what heaven might be like.

Recognizing our own Bias and Sense of Superiority

When we attempt to ignore differences (such as color of skin, or differing physical abilities) that exist between individuals, we often let our unconscious biases do the discrimination. Or, it is awkwardly acknowledged, and people give confused "what-are-you-doing-here?" type of questions while not knowing how to act normally with a person of color. On the other hand, the church must not become overly obsessed with the color of another person's skin. It is indeed a complex balance; however, as we do the hard work to become more like Jesus, we will find it more natural for us to relate to and love those who are different from us.

Perhaps one of the first steps we need to take is to stop idolizing our White North American Christian culture as having a capitalization on the blessing of God and a rich history of Christian belief. This becomes even harder when privileged Christians would have a hard time admitting this is even an idol. But, the very fact that we can't admit this, is often a sign of our own pride and sense of superiority.

I won't go too far into the weeds of this, but I wish to provide a little example of how this plays out in common privileged beliefs. For example, privileged Christians today often complain of the "increasing persecution" and hold a sentiment that wishes for the "good old days" when everyone was Christian and didn't look at you funny if you said you were. But, White American Christians may forget that in "the good old days" African American Christians were being lynched in the street, incarcerated upon accusation, and many other horrors (often by "Christians"). Or, in other places such as Canada, it may have been the "good old days" when it seemed that "everyone was a Christian;" but, all the while, where I currently reside in British Columbia, Indigenous lands were overrun, and fishing livelihoods drained away to make room for Christian immigrant farmers. How can a Christian truly long for such days? Certainly, good, even godly, things happened in those days that may be celebrated, but we cannot be ignorant of the horrors that also happened in those days to marginalized people groups – even people who professed the same faith as we do.

One simple way to assess the bias we may hold is to play a simple association game. Answer these questions with the first answer that automatically comes to mind:

- When I ask you to imagine an image of a Christian in your head, what type of person do you see? What do they look like? What type of clothes are they wearing?
- When I ask you to think of a great Christian "hero," who do you think of?
- When I ask you to imagine seeing Jesus, what does he look like?

If you're like me, or like most other privileged Christians, the automatic answer is likely: white, white, and white (among other features). There is nothing especially wrong with having those answers. But we should be aware that what our brains automatically provide for the answer to those questions tells a lot about our assumptions and biases. And, our automatic assumptions influence how we treat those around us.

It is time that White Western Christians seek to understand and be sensitive to the culture and history of those around us - understanding that Christian does not mean White, evangelical, and conservative (not to say that a Christian cannot be all these things). Perhaps, as an exercise in this, every time you hear the word *Christian*, think of the Central American Catholic immigrant or refugee. Or when you hear someone talk of Christian "heroes" think of Martin Luther King Jr. instead of Martin Luther. Or when you think of Jesus, think of a Middle Eastern, brown-skinned man instead of a white man with flowing, dirty-blond flowing hair.

In fact, the Christian center of the world is shifting from the West to the South where Latin America and Africa are populated with more Christians than the Western world combined. Phillip Jenkins projects that by 2050, only about one-fifth of all Christians in the world will be non-Hispanic Whites. Furthermore, he says that "soon, the phrase 'a white Christian' might be as mildly surprising as 'a Swedish Buddhist.'"[9] The global picture of what it is to be a Christian is much larger than the average Westerner probably thinks. Cultivating such a global perspective allows us to see where we fit in the body of Christ. One of our problems is that when we don't see from a global perspective, we will most likely see our stream of Christianity as the whole body of Christ – and as a result, we don't understand where we fit in the global body of Christ.

In a way, the privileged church is in a bubble where the global church is largely unacknowledged and where there is a perception that Christianity revolves around the West. When in a bubble, our surroundings are warped by contours and fluidity of the culture that we were raised in. This bubble often results in many misunderstandings of other people groups that often result in unhealthy biases. It also means that we tend to stick with others that are in the same bubble as us. This bubble needs to be popped before we can really see the world through the eyes of Christ.

The fact that the privileged church has a cultural bubble such as this isn't unique; every person in the world has their own cultural bubble that might skew the way they see the world. Particularly, such bubbles have created difficulty in race relations in America and other countries. Further, a common result of these bubbles is that we are unable to see people as God intends us to see them. This doesn't just mean that we have difficulties connecting with people of different cultures or races, it means that we have difficulty connecting with anyone who may be different than us in any way – cultural or racial identity, personality type, socioeconomic status, educational attainment, and the such. The vision of Christ is that the bubble would be popped, the veil removed from our eyes, and that we would see others through his eyes. When this veil is removed, we not only see our neighbors better, but we also see Christ more clearly.

The Opportunity of Diversity

The privilege of the West is evidenced by people coming from all nations and tongues to our very countries. As a result, our regional church has more opportunity to be diverse and, therefore, has a unique opportunity to magnify Christ's image in the world. It is the opportunity to live out the prophetic visions of old where people of every tongue and nation unite and worship God as one. It is truly beautiful. To neglect this gift, would be a shame.

With this in mind, the privileged body of Christ has the opportunity and calling to model cross-cultural relationships to the world. However, we all too often do not want such diversity; our churches naturally segregate based on our races, cultures, and socioeconomic statuses. And, honestly, this "segregation" makes it easier for churches to get along – after all, it is much easier to connect to and understand those who have the same cultural and socioeconomic upbringing as us. However, we should not just settle for what comes natural or easy – we should strive for what glorifies God the most.

Simply put, living in diversity will not be easy or natural (but, remember, we're called to die to ourselves!). It also won't be clean; it is bound to be messy. But – even though it might be counterintuitive – a certain type of messiness might be an indicator that the church is healthy. Such a messy, healthy church is a church where people of all kinds can get together, know they're going to make mistakes, and grow together. A healthy church is a gracious community that provides a safe place to make mistakes and grow together.

A diverse church will be a church with the crippled, blind, autistic, those with special needs, the homeless, rich, middle class, sinners, saints, alcoholics, smokers, prostitutes, Black, White, Brown, tax collectors, divorcees, lifelong married, singles, old, young etc. Do you see what I mean by messy?* But those were the very people that

---

*Not to say that a group of monotones can't be messy in of themselves. It just goes to show that even having everything in common can't be enough to overcome the difficulty that comes through different relationships.

surrounded Jesus in his day; don't you think it should be the same people who surround Jesus today?

Wholeness of Community

In current times, there has been much written and discussed about the shrinking or "death" of White Christianity as we know it in the Western world. This impending "death" has induced a hysteria where more "fundamentalist" beliefs are embraced and individuals get sucked into posturing themselves for a culture war - through which, privileged Christianity has alienated themselves from the Christianity practiced by minorities. What is more shocking is how this has even seeped into the political arena where Christians often embrace anti-immigrant policies and belligerent behavior. Need I say any more?

This growing polarization doesn't just express itself in explicit ways, but in subtle patterns of thought on the end of the privileged and a greater feeling of alienation on the end of the underprivileged. Polarization and division are not God's desire for the church, for unity is the image of God we are to portray amidst these changing dynamics and demographics.

Specifically, I strongly feel that the privileged ought to be the ones to extend a hand to the underprivileged; but, all too often we wait for the underprivileged to extend a hand to us. As privileged people, I feel that it is our God given responsibility to reach out to those who are underprivileged – whether that be economically, physically, educationally, or culturally. By reaching across the divide and embracing diversity, we fulfill the law of Christ and become representations of God's image in the world.

At the beginning of the chapter, we talked about how the Christian community is "supposed to be a breeding ground for Christlikeness" and that Christlikeness looks like the bearing of sin accompanied by proactive love and nonviolent resistance to the Cycle of Violence. If the Christian community produces such an opportunistic environment, a vastly diverse Christian community produces all the more opportunity.

Every human uniquely bears God's image in a way that others cannot. And if we all uniquely reflect God's image, much can be learned from diversity of many kinds. We have much to learn about God simply by knowing other human beings. One inevitable result of existence is the influence of others on whom one becomes. Spending a significant amount of time with another individual will almost always result in becoming more alike. In this sense, the image of God, as reflected in our neighbor, may also begin to reflect in us; thus, we more fully represent the image of God. Community refines us to make us more like God.

However, if we gather together in churches with people who think like us, act like us, have like us, and look like us - it becomes easy and comfortable because it doesn't challenge us very much. We segregate because we are less bound to face challenges from people who are similar to us. We humans tend to find the easiest way through life - we find people that agree with us to be our friends, we watch TV shows that affirm our already made opinions, and we read books that we already agree with. Yet, God, in granting each unique person a unique image of God, endorses each of our complex differences as *good*.

Diversity of Denomination

Furthermore, this concept doesn't just have to be applied on differences between individuals but can also be applied on a larger level. One could even go so far as to say that every denominational stream of the Christian faith reflects God's image in their own special way. The Catholic in consistent ethics and global presence, the Orthodox in their emphasis on tradition, the Pentecostal in their practice of the gifts of the Spirit, the Evangelicals in their dedication to the word, etc.

There is unity among different denominational streams in that the person of Christ is central to them all, but there is not uniformity among different denominations. This lack of uniformity has been used to draw lines between the denominations and force people to pick sides when this lack of uniformity is to be used to make the global church more whole. But, since we often force people to pick sides, we end up with Christians living in their own isolated denominational echo chambers in which we see some churches being completely compromised because they have so completely lost the call of Christ.

Loving Unity vs. Tolerance

The Christian virtue of loving unity amidst vast differences is God's plan for how conceivably irreconcilable differences are to be reconciled between individuals. This is also attempted by the secular virtue of *tolerance*. I have wondered why such a word was chosen as the word to represent a virtue that is meant to bring world peace. After all, tolerance seems to have negative connotations in that to "tolerate" another individual implies that they are doing something annoying that we must attempt to ignore. If

Christians were to only "tolerate" others in the body of Christ - what an ignoble goal that would be! It's as if the world didn't think that such loving unity was possible, and that we might as well settle for mere tolerance of those we disagree with.

Jesus sets a higher standard: one that doesn't just tolerate their neighbor but lifts them up and acknowledges their inherent dignity. Further, the concept of tolerance, as it is used today, means that one must acknowledge that everyone has an equal claim to truth and that no one has a monopoly on truth. But, accepting such a "virtue" means ignoring irreconcilable differences of belief in order to create a sort of "peace" between people. But, when we accept two contradicting beliefs as equally true, it doesn't produce peace, but confusion. The ethic of Jesus cries out that everyone is worthy of dignity because they are simply humans made in God's image. The ethic of the world insists that everyone is worthy of the "dignity to be tolerated" because there is no truth. The ethic of Jesus insists that everyone is worthy of sacrificial love aimed in their direction. He insists that we love our neighbor, not just tolerate our neighbor. Jesus calls us to love our neighbor even if what they believe is completely different from what we believe. Jesus insists on a humility rooted in truth that serves others no matter their ideological differences from us.

What's more, the world says, "can't we all just tolerate our enemies?" Jesus responds, *No, that is not enough. You must love your enemies and pray for those who persecute you.*[10] Tolerance is certainly a weak attempt at peace compared to the love of Jesus that goes *all in* to validate the worth of every individual.

To be clear, Christlike diversity isn't one of difference for the sake of difference. This diversity is one of difference *for the sake of wholeness* – for the sake of completeness. If the church is full of people who are the same, the image of Christ will be limited. When diversity is embraced, Christ's body is more Christlike. *Many members, one body.* If we succumb to diversity for the sake of diversity, we may succumb to accepting diverse beliefs without critical analysis of those beliefs. This creates a very shallow community, as beliefs are reduced to fluff for the sake of diversity. We must not settle for accepting contradictions within the body, but we also must be aware that many things that appear to be contradictions often are not. Diversity is not a fluffy, easy dream, but one that comes with much challenge and humble wrestling. This is to be discussed in more detail in the next chapter.

Love Your Enemies

Unity amidst diversity results in growth, but it is a growth that comes through many difficulties. Martin Luther King made this same plea when asking his fellow White pastors to support the cause of civil rights; he said, "There is a constructive nonviolent tension that is necessary for growth."[11] Growth, no doubt, comes through challenge and tension, and we will never grow if we are never challenged. Therefore, the monochrome church stagnates in its growth, it is not challenged, and its members do not become more Christlike. Jesus said,

> *If you only love those who love you, why should you get credit for that? Even sinners love those who love them! And if you do good only to*

*those who do good to you, why should you get
credit? Even sinners do that much! And if you
lend money only to those who can repay you,
why should you get credit? Even sinners will
lend to other sinners for a full return.* (Luke
6:32-34 NLT)

In that same sentiment, I think one could say, "It's easy
to love those who are similar to us. What is that credit to
you? Don't we all have an easy time getting along with
those who are similar to us? Even sinners get along with
those that are like them." Or, "*if you greet only your own people,
what more are you doing than others? Even the pagans do that?*"
(Matthew 5:47). If we are only friends primarily with those
who come from the same race, social status, or intellectual
ability as us, then Jesus says we are *no different than pagans.*

Love is more profound when it crosses barriers. Jesus says,
"love your enemies," - that is how the Christian is supposed
to live. It is *one* thing when people love those who are like
them; it is a *whole other* thing to love people that are different
from them; but, it is certainly a *divine* thing to love our
enemies. Yet, so many Christians find it all too easy to stop
at the first one. Or worse still, after stopping there, they go
so far as to think that those who are different from them are
their enemies (i.e., the immigrant, the progressive, the
conservative, the LGBTQ+, etc.) What good is it if you only
love those who are like you? Did not Hitler "love" his fellow
Germans? Real Christian love exists among diverse people
who wouldn't normally get along but are brought together
in common unity in their love for Christ. I am convinced
that this is why Jesus said that *the world will know we are
Christians by our love for one another.*[12] In the disciple's day,
the churches would be made up of Jews and Gentiles -

groups that historically had animosity toward one another. So, when they came together in the church it was profound enough for the outsider to say, "It surely must be the love of God that is working among these people."

This idea of love is not just a *nice* idea that we passively try to affirm, though. Love is a toil. Love is work. *Love is longsuffering.*[13] The love that the world will recognize as Christian love is a love that is impossible without divine intervention. When I walk into some churches, the "love" I see is no different than the "love" that one sees in the country club. This, by no means, distinguishes Christian love from the world's love. They will know we are Christians by our love when Palestinians and Israelites, Germans and Jews, Hutus and Tutsis, Aboriginals and Australians, Blacks and Whites, Catholics and Protestants, even Republicans and Democrats, worship together, share lives together, and stand hand-in-hand in love for one another and in love for Christ. Then, will the world witness this and say, "This could only be the love of God!" Through our radical love for those who are different from us and even our enemies, the world looks at the Church and truly sees God for who he is. *God is a God of redeemed relationships.*

Gracism

By embracing diversity, the church truly becomes the body of Christ. Paul, in his classic description of the body in 1 Corinthians 12, lays forth a vision for what this looks like. David A. Anderson, in his book, *Gracism*[14], dives into this passage and points out how we are to read this passage. Paul begins the discussion on the body by stating that all are baptized into *one body* – *"whether Jews or Greeks"* (referring to race and culture) *"whether slave or free"* (referring to class).

It is in an embrace of diversity of race, culture, and class that the body receives many of its body parts. I join with Anderson in admonishing you to keep this context of race, culture, and class when you read the passage:

> The human body has many parts, but the many parts make up one whole body. So it is with the body of Christ. Some of us are Jews, some are Gentiles, some are slaves, and some are free. But we have all been baptized into one body by one Spirit, and we all share the same Spirit. Yes, the body has many different parts, not just one part. If the foot says, "I am not a part of the body because I am not a hand," that does not make it any less a part of the body. And if the ear says, "I am not part of the body because I am not an eye," would that make it any less a part of the body? If the whole body were an eye, how would you hear? Or if your whole body were an ear, how would you smell anything? But our bodies have many parts, and God has put each part just where he wants it. How strange a body would be if it had only one part! Yes, there are many parts, but only one body. The eye can never say to the hand, "I don't need you." The head can't say to the feet, "I don't need you." In fact, some parts of the body that seem weakest and least important are actually the most necessary. And the parts we regard as less

> honorable are those we clothe with the
> greatest care. So we carefully protect
> those parts that should not be seen, while
> the more honorable parts do not require
> this special care. So God has put the body
> together such that extra honor and care
> are given to those parts that have less
> dignity. This makes for harmony among
> the members, so that all the members care
> for each other. If one part suffers, all the
> parts suffer with it, and if one part is
> honored, all the parts are glad. All of you
> together are Christ's body, and each of
> you is a part of it. (1 Corinthians 12:12-27
> NLT)

Indeed, we see this passage through new eyes when reading it in this context. To be clear, Paul is talking about the gifts and callings that each are given as well as the different classes, cultures, and races that make up the church (many kinds of diversity). It is in this diversity that God is magnified.

What's more, Paul says that those who *seem weakest are the most necessary.* Or, we could even say, *the most important?* Even though it may seem unfair, God seems to have a special place in his heart for the weaker and poor amongst humanity. Such a theme is found throughout scripture. It's not that God has favorites, but that God perhaps sees the weaker as more deserving of the blessing of God; or, as already possessing the blessing of God, for *blessed, currently, are the poor.* Therefore, we are to adopt the same heart of God for the least of these and treat them with special honor and lift them up.

Furthermore, we cover those who are more vulnerable among us. It means that we *give extra honor and care* to such individuals. For example, if you were a White person in an African American church, you would be much more vulnerable than if you were in an all-white church. You may have the attention of more people and are more vulnerable to embarrassment. Even a trip in the hallway might be enough to embarrass one in such a situation. Thus, when we have one who is vulnerable among us, we treat such people with extra care, grace, and honor.

In a sense, Jesus is concerned with equality and that those who are low would be lifted up and that those who are high would be brought lower. This allows for harmony and unity amidst such vast differences to the point that we enter into each other's lives. We rejoice with those who rejoice, and we suffer with those who suffer. We grieve with our brothers and sisters whose homeland is in the thick of civil war and violence. We rejoice with our brothers and sisters as they celebrate people and places that are dear to their hearts. We enter into each other's experience and share in emotions that wouldn't naturally be our own. This oneness amidst diversity is truly what it means to be Christ's body.

Communion: A Practice in Oneness

When Jesus first called his disciples, they were a group of individuals one would not expect to see together. A few fishermen (common laborers), a tax collector (someone who worked for the oppressive government and benefited from it), and a zealot (someone who wanted to kill those who worked for the government and overthrow them). Jesus brought people from all walks of life together and journeyed with them for three years. After those three years, no doubt, these twelve disciples were very close to one another. Three years of spending every day together, traveling together, and eating together.

Those three years came to a pinnacle on the Passover meal – the last supper. Jesus addressed his disciples, *"I have been eagerly waiting to have this Passover meal with you. It'll be my last meal until the kingdom of God arrives."* Then, he took the bread, and he broke it – *"This is my body given for you; do this in remembrance of me."* Then he took the cup – *"This cup is the new covenant in my blood, which is poured out for you."*[15]

Communion is now something that Christians partake in regularly and it reminds us of Christ's body broken for our sins and his blood poured out for our redemption. It is a reminder that Christ totally gave himself for others and a call for us to do the same. In communion, we join with Christ in his death so that we may join with him in his resurrection. One of the classic scriptures on communion is found in Paul's first letter to the Corinthians. Paul exhorts, *your meeting together as church is doing more harm than good. There are divisions among you. What's more, when you come together, you are not eating the Lord's Supper; for when you eat, you each bring your own private suppers for yourselves. In such, one person goes hungry while another is getting drunk and fat. Why do you despise the body of Christ by humiliating those who have nothing? When you come together, some having too much and some too little, you are sinning against the very blood and body of the Lord – making a mockery of what Jesus did for you. Examine yourself before you eat and drink the Lord's Supper, lest you keep casting judgement on yourselves.*[16]

Communion is the place where all Christians, regardless of their privilege, life situation, and race, come together and proclaim, "We are one in Christ." When this is undermined by divisions and selfishness, the Lord's Table ceases to be the Lord's Table.

The Lord's Supper entails a certain amount of sharing and love among those who partake in it. When we fail to look after the poor and needy among us while enjoying the pleasures of privilege, we are unworthy of partaking in communion with Christ or with our neighbor. *Examine yourself before you eat and drink the Lord's supper, lest you cast judgement on yourself.*

For the Jew (and almost every other ethnic group on earth), to share a meal with another person is a sacred sign of fellowship and brotherhood. The simple human act of eating with another individual is an act that entails intimacy and friendship. A meal is rarely, if ever, held with one's enemies, but is eaten on a regular basis with one's friends and family. It is fitting that a meal would become the ritual that encourages and builds up the church – reminding us why we come together. A meal centered around the saving act of Jesus' humility and authority aimed at our own redemption. When we eat, we celebrate our liberation from sin and the restoration of human fellowship through the body and blood of Christ. Gustavo Gutierrez writes, "it is a memorial of Christ which presupposes an ever-renewed acceptance of the meaning of his life - a total giving to others."[17] In communion, we are reminded of how, even while we were still sinners, Christ communed with us and gave himself to us; from which we enter into a life marked by communion in which we commune with one another and give ourselves to one another.

Sadly, I feel like many of us in the Western world miss out on the profoundness of communion partly because we have distilled it down to a measly crumb and a shot of grape juice when it was meant to be a whole meal. I wonder how many Christian communities would be transformed if they committed to eating a meal together each week; or better yet, ate the Lord's Supper every week. After all, that is only the natural thing for a family to do.

7

DIVERSITY AND DIFFICULTY

Unity is not an event accomplished once and for all, but something which is always in the process of becoming, something which is achieved with courage and freedom of spirit, sometimes at the price of painful, heart-rending decisions.

Gustavo Gutierrez [1]

The Challenges of Diversity

Since diversity within community is something that reflects the image of God more fully to the world, diversity is something to be celebrated and pursued. God is magnified by the diversity of his church.

The Christian is often asked what the purpose of the Christian life is. A common answer is *to glorify God.* If this is true, the next question invariably is, how does one glorify God? As evident in this discussion, one way of doing this is to pursue diversity within the church. Too often we fill our churches with people of the same color, same economic standing, and same doctrine. We have our White churches, Black churches, Asian churches, our hundreds of denominations, our homeless ministries, and our extravagant churches, often, all neatly separated from one another. And, often our separation from each other is excused by "doctrinal differences," or differences in belief or emphasis. But, certainly, we should all probably agree that the doctrine of unity and community is more important than many of the beliefs that separate churches.

Don't get me wrong, doctrine is important, but it must be admitted that many of the hills we've chose to die upon are silly and nonessential when cared to unity. Paul wrote to Titus telling him to "avoid foolish controversies, genealogies, dissensions, and quarrels about the law, for they are unprofitable and worthless." He goes onto say that one should "have nothing more to do with" such a person who continually threatens unity. This is because the church should be devoted to good works, not to the fine print.[2] When many different people come together, there is more potential for disagreements, but we must not let these differences become a reason to segregate our churches.

Is not God more glorified when we worship him together in diversity than when we worship him separately in our own monotone groups? Often when diverse groups worship together, some may say that they are able to worship God "despite" their differences. Let this not be the case! God is worshipped, in part, through our diversity, not despite it. It is not enough to be a diverse community, though.

Even so, diversity is bound to challenge unity. Even the early church faced such a challenge rooted in the cultural divide between Jews and Gentiles. The heated debate was about whether the Gentiles could really be Christians if they hadn't been circumcised. Disagreement often requires compromise. Sometimes this means that we accommodate to those we disagree with because it won't make that much of a difference, or we lay down the issue for the sake of unity. For example, Paul convinced Timothy (a son of a Gentile) to get circumcised so that it would not hinder their ministry to the Jews.[3] Such a compromise on Timothy's end required much humility to do something he felt wasn't necessary, but for the sake of church unity he did something painful. Or, in time, Paul was able to get the pro-circumcision Jews to accept uncircumcised Gentiles as their brothers and sisters, for, in Christ, "only faith working through love" counts for anything.[4] No doubt, some were upset by this decision, but for the sake of unity and Christian love, it was written off as a non-essential to the faith. I'm sure that to many of the Jewish Christians of the time, circumcision was as important to them as baptism is to the majority of Christians today. How many of the arguments that divide churches are less significant than this?

Grace and Truth

Since diversity creates such challenges, unity amidst diversity is all the more God-endowed. However, the desire for a diverse and loving community can bring the temptations to compromise on truth for the sake of "unity." We have seen this in the last couple decades where community is elevated above truth, Jesus is reduced to a great teacher, accompanied by a gospel without Jesus at the center. Yet, in doing so, false unity emerges, for there may not unity in belief of the divinity of Christ; and Christianity is reduced to a humanistic vision of world peace. Diversity must not compromise truth. Yet, the answer is not to compromise diversity, these points of contention must be wrestled with in the Christian community, ensuring that truth and grace kiss.

How do we accept people of many backgrounds and theological beliefs without compromising on truth? Are there certain things that people need to agree on to be a part of the Christian community, and where does that line get drawn? These questions must be evaluated with wisdom.

Diversity challenges truth (for compromising truth may be a means to embrace a wide range of diversity), and diversity may challenge individuals (for it is usually more difficult to thrive with individuals different from ourselves). This has contributed to the widening divide between the Christian right and Christian left. The right has often failed to embrace diversity resulting in monotone churches with hardline beliefs that "ensure" it will be on the side of "truth" at the expense of grace – often appearing in the form of ultra-conservative churches. On the other hand, the left has often done a wonderful job embracing diversity while compromising truth for the sake of grace. It takes on the challenge of diversity to the extreme, but as a result, truth is challenged to the point where it no longer has a foundation. Both the rejection of grace for the sake of truth and the rejection of truth for the sake of grace are actions that prevent a church from being the living body of Christ.

In an overly simplistic sense, it seems that the Right considers truth to be foundational to the church while the Left considers gracious community to be the foundation of the church. Yet, a Biblical worldview emphasizes that both are extremely important for the church. We must live in the awkward middle between the Left and the Right and stand for diversity *and* truth within community.

In one instance, Paul calls the community of God, "the pillar and foundation of the truth."[5] The community of the people of God are the foundation that the truth stands on, the pillar that holds truth in place. Truth does not stand on doctrinal statements; it stands on the community of Christ. If the church isn't the living body of Christ in loving community, then truth has no pillar to stand on. Only when the church is the loving body of Christ does truth stand. Truth without Christian community is like a roof without a building to cover it. Yet, similarly, a community without truth is like a building without a roof! Therefore, the body of Christ must cling to truth and cling to Christian community. If one or the other is lost, then the church is like a roof that lays on the ground, or a building without a roof to shelter it.

Drawing the Line

Diversity is a word that has the potential to be controversial in today's conservative culture. Taken to its extreme, the concept of "embracing diversity" can create wrong representation of who Jesus is to the world. For example, one might be tempted to embrace other religions as adding to diversity that magnifies the image of God in the world. However, Christ would have to be denied for such an all-inclusive philosophy because such a philosophy would necessarily include aspects that are antithetical to the person of Christ. Thus, there must be a point that a line is drawn as to what should be included. However, it does not seem the Christian world will agree upon such a line anytime soon - that is one reason there are so many denominations (a valid reason, among many silly reasons). I do not wish to tell the reader where I think the line should be drawn, but that people on either side of the line should have enough humility to admit that they might not have all the answers - as long as the person of Christ is not compromised.

Some say it is dangerous to boil down the Christian faith into what one would call "essential beliefs." Such leads to questions like, is all that matters the virgin birth, the crucifixion, and the resurrection? I would like to propose that the gospel is much simpler than such questions. What if the illiterate, simple-minded, man who understands that God became human and redeemed him, now calls on the Lord for salvation? And, in his joy, is baptized and shares with his neighbors the good news. All that man believes is all that we must believe as Christians. It has nothing to do with intellectual assent to doctrinal positions and everything to do with simply receiving the simple grace of God in our hearts and letting it flow through oneself. If it is anything other than that, then you have had too much time to sit around and think (not to mean that thinking is wrong, but to emphasize that sitting around is wrong). Christ is primary, many other details are secondary. Again, Paul says that *"The only thing that counts* is faith expressing itself through love."[6]

I do not wish to reject doctrine or the details of Christian life (for I adore these details), but to look at the bigger picture of what God is doing in the world. If we get caught up in the details, we may miss the big picture. The secondary details *can be important* because they allow us to live a more intellectual and thoughtful Christian life. Such details add to the richness of our faith, and such details may be important because they have implications for how we live. Yet, we can know those details and hold them to be true without living into Christ's kingdom. It is the age old "battle" of grace vs. truth, when it is not to be a battle at all. The Christian life is to be a marriage of grace and truth. We must have grace enough to admit that we don't have it all figured out and admit that we don't know exactly how God intends certain passages of scripture to be interpreted. We must have truth enough to see what is obvious and emphasized in scripture. And, when we are in doubt about such things, we must remember that "mercy triumphs over judgement."[7]

Christianity as a Person

Many approach the Christian life like it is a textbook (as laid out in the Bible), thinking that everything is laid out for them so that they don't have to discover what the Christian life is for themselves; but, the Christian life is not a textbook, it is a person – Jesus Christ. When we start seeing Jesus as a person, our whole perspective changes. Jesus is a person, and each Christian has a unique relationship with him. It follows that there is no single way to approach and communicate with Jesus - each must cultivate their own relationship with him. When we live life trying to know Jesus only by learning about him, we will never truly know him. For, to know a person, one must live in some sort of communion with them. And, as we spend time with him, we will become more like him.

In using the "textbook-approach," Jesus is viewed from a distance and is interacted with as if he were a painting at a museum, or even more shameful, the description of a painting that is beside it. We look at him, admire him, talk about him, praise him, but from a distance - forgetting that he is living and active among us as our friend, Lord, and Savior. We can get so caught up in doctrinal statements about who Jesus was - the Son of God, a part of the Trinity, fully God, fully human, etc. - that we can forget that everything about Jesus has profound implications for our life. Sometimes we get so caught up in doctrinal statements that *Jesus himself is reduced to statements.* Just as a piece of art loses its fulness when reduced to descriptive words, the descriptive words can sometimes even mischaracterize the painting or the description misunderstood. Therefore, I urge you not to get caught up in doctrinal statements or debates and use such statements as they were meant to be used: to understand the person of Jesus better while acknowledging that there is much more to be known about Christ - And not just to know *about* him, but to really *know* him as your personal friend, Father, and Lord.

Jesus was never meant to be just looked at, admired, talked about, or even just praised; Jesus came to be Emmanuel, "God with us," every day intimately intertwined with our very being. We are not just looking at a painting; we are pulled into the "painting" of Jesus, projecting a grand picture of the kingdom of heaven. So, when we look at the perfection of Jesus, we too are drawn into that perfection. When we look at the humility of Jesus, we are drawn into that humility. When we look at his life, death, love, passion, suffering, joy, and all that he lives, we are drawn into that! That is the Christian life - to be drawn into the person of Christ and be transformed into his image, an image that is living and active in the world.

From here arises a call to simple, basic Christianity in which what is obvious and emphasized is what we focus on and devote themselves to. Along these lines, I have hope that Christianity around the world will become more focused on the "basics" and that our primary goal will be to simply love people and work toward God's kingdom. A world where Christ is central. A Christianity where denominational lines aren't battle lines, but are simply markers of the diversity within the body of Christ; where the Catholic works alongside the Protestant. For, helping people see Jesus is more important than arguments that are found in the details. Perhaps this is a lofty dream, but I believe this is one of the great gifts that may come with this next generation of believers - where there is less care for the denomination and more care for the person of Christ.

I believe all these religious debates became a problem partly because Christianity has become so "privileged" in the West, that people have time to start arguing over the details. But, in other countries where persecution prevails, the believers join together common unity in Christ, because each other is all they have. What really matters tends to come to the surface among dire situations. And what matters can be lost when we live in such a comfortable situation. One only needs to read the Old Testament prophets to understand the dangers of comfort and prosperity – or, better yet, the words of Jesus.

Current Challenges

We are to keep the person of Jesus at the center and not let differences get in the way of unity and, instead, allow our differences to glorify God. Still, there are many issues in the world today that create difficulties for the church. To be clear, these "difficulties" are not bad for the church; but, I contend that they are good for the church. For, challenge should lead to growth if we receive the challenge in a Christlike manner. If we don't receive such challenges in a Christlike manner, these challenges will make us fearful, combative, bitter, and unloving.

As already stated, the difficulty is the push for the church to include ideas and lifestyles that may or may not go against traditional Christian belief. On one side, there is a push for acceptance of all lifestyles and behavior to the point where sin may be condoned or encouraged. In doing so, sin is not called sin and we think, 'can't we just let people live they want to live?' While some ask these questions, fundamentalists draw a hard line in the sand and pronounce condemnation upon the other side. This is a cycle that does not produce Christlike love on either side of the line. We must learn how to break this cycle if we are ever to truly achieve Christlike diversity.

There are many other moral and justice[*] issues that need to be addressed in the church today (i.e., assisted suicide, euthanasia, immigration values, war, abortion, etc.), but we will limit ourselves to a short discussion on sexuality, since it directly relates to the concept of diversity within our communities.

Sexuality

Sexuality is a topic that the church has evidently been unable to address appropriately. Whether it be the pedophilia crisis in the catholic church or the "purity culture" movements in Protestant churches, the Christian church has massively failed at having a Christlike

---

[*] Throughout this book, I have mostly discussed what some would consider "justice" issues. This chapter is set aside to, more or less, address the "moral" issues that the church faces. However, I would like to note that every moral issue is also a justice issue and vice-versa. For some reason, the privileged church has seemingly separated moral and justice issues; often putting more effort in discussion of the "moral" issues and ignoring the "justice" issues. To me, it is weird of us to have done this. Perhaps it's because the "justice" issues make us uncomfortable with our privilege while we can keep a safe distance when discussing "moral issues." For this reason, I won't go too in depth about "moral" issues, but only discuss one as an example of how we are to treat others. There are plenty of other good books that cover such topics in depth.

worldview as it pertains to sexuality; and, consequently, the burden of these failures have largely fallen on the vulnerable, disadvantaged, and underprivileged (i.e., children, women, and members of the LGBTQIA2S+ community). Such failures ought to cause us to approach the topic of sexuality with incredible humility, but, many churches have tried to make up for these failures by becoming even more law-oriented and drawing even bolder lines between *us* and *them*. Yet, by doing so, we are only trying to fix our problems with the very methods that caused them in the first place.

The current area where the church seems most inadequate is in our view and handling of LGBTQ+ issues. In America, there is perhaps no other identity group which the church has done more harm to. The church has shamed those of diverse sexualities and have singled them out as "worse sinners" than anyone else. I honestly do not think I could emphasize enough how much harm the church has done to this community and how much harm this has done to the witness of Christ. This is certainly one of the deepest sins the church has committed, and we must eagerly and humbly seek forgiveness. Sadly, much of the church is still in denial of this sin.

With this being the current condition of the church, many who are reading this may feel anxious or cringe every time I use the word, *diversity*. Perhaps that is the appropriate response to the word, for we are, indeed, more comfortable in our own clearly defined bubbles. What matters is whether we are letting that initial response of anxiety lead to immediate defensiveness or a willingness to humbly wrestle. If it is met with defensiveness, we will inevitably continue to make the same mistakes. If it is met with a willingness to wrestle, we will certainly make new mistakes, but, at least, we will certainly grow. To wrestle and consider that we may be wrong in some of these areas seems to be the humblest way to respond.

First off, as I have mentioned previously, I'd like to emphasize that *responsibility lies with the privileged to be the ones who reach out to the underprivileged.* In the instance of sexuality, it is evident that those who do not fall into the traditional categories of sexuality and gender are the ones who are the underprivileged. And to be clear, the LGBTQ+ Christian is not underprivileged because of anything that is wrong with them, but they are underprivileged in the way that the Christian church has shunned, rejected, and silenced their voices. Therefore, I truly believe that the hate, unkindness, condemnation, and sin that has resulted from this controversy falls majorly upon the privileged – those within "mainstream" conservative Christianity who have treated the LGBTQ+ as outcasts and untouchables. If such a spirit of exclusion can thrive in the church, one must seriously question if we are truly being like Christ.

So, to return to the question at hand, if we can say that diverse denominations, diverse races, diverse cultures, diverse talents, and diverse languages magnify the image of God, then why not say that diverse sexual orientations also magnify God's image? A traditional Christian ethic would indeed say that they do magnify God's image, for "male and female he created them, in the image of God he created *them.*" Surely a female bears God's image in a way that a male cannot, and a male in ways a female cannot. But what about those who identify with the LGBTQ+ community?

On a personal note, I have honestly wrestled with this question for many years. I grew up in a home that unquestionably considered such lifestyles to be wrong; yet, as I have had Christian friends come out as gay – the reality of this belief has demanded a certain amount of humble wrestling as opposed to distant indifference.

This question is further complicated by the fact that there is a scientifically proven propensity for people to be born biologically inclined to adhere to nontraditional sexual lifestyles. Surely, people are "born gay." Therefore, the traditional argument that such desires are merely a "choice" break down against the weight of evidence. Furthermore, if we can say that the image of God in which people of color are born into is perfect; why would the image of God in which LGBTQ+ people are born into be any different?

There is indeed brokenness within creation that results in a less than optimal human condition. We are all broken in one way or another; but, it is no small thing to label another as "more broken than we are." And, even if one were to label LGBTQ+ individuals as "more broken," a Christlike approach would entail having *more* compassion, *more* patience, *more* love, and *more* humility in such relationships. For, we are to *bear with the failings of the weak.*[8]

However, I choose not this route of thinking. I think the humbler approach is not to label certain people as "more broken" than other individuals. Instead of ordering people on a hierarchy of brokenness, it seems more fitting to identify my brokenness with the common brokenness of those around me and allow that to be a gateway into community.

I do not intend this chapter to become a debate on the Christian case for the rightness or wrongness of the LGBTQ+ lifestyle (there are many other better books for that); but, in the spirit of full disclosure, I have come to the conclusion that it is near impossible to fully and truly love an LGBTQ+ person unless one embraces the individual for all they are – gender identity and all. Therefore, I think the highest virtue, Christian love, takes precedence and precludes us from condemning and our fellow LGBTQ+ people as "worse than" or singled-out sinners.

Yet, even if one believes an LGBTQ+ lifestyle is a sin, the answer is not to exclude our LGBTQ+ neighbors. In fact, much can be learned from these individuals, especially as we strive to love and understand anyone who may have differing lifestyles and views from our own. If Jesus thought loving our enemies would be good for us, we can surely, at least, love those who are different than us!

More so, I would say it is extremely arrogant for one to say that a practicing LGBTQ+ individual cannot be a Christian. Jesus himself looks at the heart, and not on outward appearances. In fact, I think heaven will be populated with people who were perceived as some of the worst people on earth, while missing many people we thought were shoo-ins for heaven. I'm sure many of us will get to heaven, see who Jesus is hanging out with, and pharasitically say, "Don't you know what type of sinner you are breaking bread with?" Thus, we repeat the exact words and motivation of the pharisees who condemned Jesus for breaking bread with "sinners."

Embracing diversity as it relates to sexuality, means that we embrace the diverse individual as an image of God. We don't have to completely agree with their lifestyle (as I don't agree with most other privileged Christian lifestyles); yet, we cannot truly love others while seeing them *primarily* as "sinners" Embracing them means meeting them where they are and leaving our own preconceived notions of "who they should be" at the door.

Embracing them as individuals means we become comfortable spending time with them and supporting them in who they are made to be. Jesus seemed to be most comfortable spending time with the sexually immoral, cheaters, and sinners. I think, as Christians, we have been all too uncomfortable around LGBTQ+ individuals. Often, Christians may get awkward, have a difficult time looking at them, avoid them, and maybe even feel disgusted at their lifestyle. We are blessed that this is not how Jesus saw us! In the eyes of Jesus, each man is a sinner, yet he does not wince, avert his gaze, or even have a stirring awkwardness. On the cross, Jesus gazed at us in all our sin, took it on himself, and identified himself with a sinful humanity. *Jesus came to save sinners of whom I am the worst.*

It seems that Jesus was most comfortable when he was with sinners. On the other hand, it seems that Jesus was most uncomfortable around religious people – where he might end up flipping tables or saying offensive things toward them.[9] In reflection of Jesus, we must become comfortable with our LGBTQ+ neighbor and love them as an image of God.

We also must also remember that identity is not found in our sexuality – our culture has become so obsessed with "finding our identity" that it gets associated with things we were never intended to find our identity in. Our identity is to be ultimately defined by God as being made in the image of God and being his dearly loved children. If we look at our LGBTQ+ neighbor, and we primarily identify them as being "sinners," then we have not yet begun to see through the eyes of Christ. In Christ, all identifications and categories given to people must fade away – when we look at people, we don't identify them primarily with their profession, sexuality/gender, social status, culture, disability, race, or, much less, their sin! We must primarily see them as images of God, fearfully and wonderfully made.

For, "There is neither Jew nor Gentile, neither slave nor free, nor is there male and female, for you are all one in Christ Jesus. If you belong to Christ, then you are Abraham's seed, and heirs according to the promise" (Galatians 3:28-29 NIV).

A Note on Non-Judgement

Earlier in this book, I proposed that the first command of God was not to multiply and rule (Chapter 4, *A note on fruitfulness and multiplying*). If this is so, what was the first command of God to humanity? The first command God gives to humanity comes in the second chapter of Genesis: "And the Lord God *commanded* the man, 'you are free to eat from any tree in the garden; but you must not eat from the tree of the knowledge of good and evil, for when you eat from it you will certainly die.'"[10]

We must remember that the name Satan means "accuser" in the biblical sense. If our primary means of interacting with sinners is to accuse, then we are playing the role of Satan! Greg Boyd emphasizes that the first sin of mankind was to eat from the "tree of knowledge of good and evil."[11] So, in this sense, man, in his created state, was not meant to have God's knowledge of good and evil. But, as soon as he ate the fruit, he saw good and evil and now was a bearer of judgement. The state of man laying judgement upon others for what was right and wrong was not God's intention for created humanity. Now, the church often prides itself on knowing what is right and wrong. The very thing that made us sinners in the first place is often how people define those in the church! We think our knowledge of what is good and what is evil is what makes us good, but it is, in truth, what makes us evil.

Jesus himself says, "Do not judge, or you too will be judged."[12] And this non-judgement consists of refusing to act judgmental toward another in addition to possessing a mind that does not even think judgmental thoughts. This seems to be another one of the sayings of Jesus that we don't take too seriously; some might brush it off with a quaint, "he really meant is that we aren't supposed to condemn others, but we still must tell them when they are wrong." This is what Dallas Willard calls "the gospel of sin management,"[13] and it stands opposed to the gospel of abundant life! By all means, there is such a thing as right and wrong, but *right and wrong* is not what the image of God is supposed to be defined by. Surely, we are supposed to work for the redemption of such situations and encourage others to live in a way that pleases God. But, the "rules" are never to be the defining characteristic of the Christian life (as it was for the pharisees). Instead, our ultimate focus is Jesus and allowing his life to flow through us.

Most of us wouldn't ever explicitly express our accusations to the people we are judging, but we all probably know some fellow Christians who would. We might think thoughts, give them a funny look, or express judgement about another to a close friend, but never to their face. Either way, it is a form of accusational judgement that Jesus condemns. Every accusation and judgement we make is the very way the devil works in the world.

When we fall into the devil's trap and start making accusations, we begin to have a god-complex that makes ourselves feel better and more righteous than those around us. But, God is the great adjudicator, and he doesn't need us to accuse in order for him to get his judgement right. He sees all the evidence without our help. Our responsibility is to love and encourage life. By spewing accusations, we are once again falling into the devil's temptation to eat from the tree of the knowledge of good and evil.

If anything, Jesus spent the majority of his time with outcasts, imparting a love that redeems and transforms. People in his day grumbled at him and said, "He has gone to be the guest of a sinner," *how foolish!*[14] People scoffed at Jesus saying, "If this man were a prophet, he would have known what sort of woman this is who is touching him, for she is a sinner."[15]But, Jesus shoved it in the face of the religious leaders and said, *I know exactly who these people are, and they are closer to the kingdom than any one of you, you brood of vipers.*[16] (Incidentally, as we have already mentioned, the only people Jesus ever accused were the religious and privileged people of his day).

Let us repent from un-Christlike judgement of our neighbor and turn to a loving Christlike compassion. Again, I think we, in the privileged church, have misunderstood what compassion looks like. We have often confused compassion with pity. Or, worse, we have confused compassion with patronization; this happens when we base our compassion on assumptions we make about people's lives. We assume we know what others need, but compassion is much deeper and humbler than our common understanding of compassion. Compassion is a willingness to enter someone's situation and "suffer with" them. Only then can we really cultivate understanding in such situations.

This does not mean that we must always approve of the way everyone lives, but that we seek to understand instead of casting judgement. "Jesus had compassion, for they were like sheep without a shepherd."[17] And often, when Jesus had such compassion and entered people's situations through radical, non-judgmental love, it was in that moment when people were redeemed and repented from their sin. Jesus was the first person since pre-fall Adam and Eve to have never eaten from *the tree of knowledge of good and evil*; his tree was the *tree of life*.

After treating people with redemptive love, Jesus would simply say, "Go, and sin no more."[18] It was a love that transformed, a love that redeemed, a love that changed people's lives. When such love was received, tax collectors paid back all the people they had ripped off[19] and adulterers became missionaries.[20] That is the kind of judgement found in Jesus, a judgment that declares that each image of God is worthy of such love. Not a judgement that proclaims, "You are a sinner going to hell and I am right," nor is it a judgment that proclaims to oneself, "I know that person is a sinner, so I will avoid contact with them."

Jesus' judgement is one whose heart is soft and receives life from the tree of life, the cross. Our judgment is of one whose heart is hard and receives its "life" from the tree of knowledge. O *Lord, make us like you, forgive us for constantly eating from the tree of knowledge of good and evil by passing judgment unto our neighbor and let us once again eat from the tree of life.*

Jesus says, "Let he who is without sin cast the first stone"[21]– to which no one may throw a stone, yet, Jesus, the sinless one, still refuses to cast the first stone. Such non-condemnation is the radical mercy of God upon the sinner. Such is the radical mercy we are to show to the world.

A Note on the Purity of the Church

Paradoxically, there should be much concern about the purity of the church if the church is to be the image of God in the world. This must mean that we reject what does not fit in the image of God, right? Yes, to some extent, but the reality is that to hold the church to strict standards of purity and living will only result in a judgmental legalistic church which excludes non-believers and, even, struggling believers. We should strive for purity within the church, but it must come with an understanding that Jesus allows the "wheat and the weeds to grow together."[22] When Jesus comes back, he will separate the sheep from the goats and all that's left will be the perfect image of Christ. In the meantime, we must be concerned with our own relationship with Christ, encourage others to live holier lives based in their relationship with Christ, and leave the judgment up to God.

Though we are to leave the judgement up to God, there is much to be said about *accountability* within the community of God. Having a countenance of non-judgement does not mean that we ignore sin. Having such a countenance allows us to approach sinners with a pure heart that only seeks to help another along their journey in following Christ. We must not use *accountability* as an excuse to cast judgement, as so many do. I could say much more about accountability, but I will simply leave it with this: accountability is the natural result of being a part of an intimate body of Christ. There are many who try to "force" accountability but doing so will only result in hurt or harm. It must be done with a pure heart amidst intimate and compassionate community.

8

REDEEMING HUMANITY

When we lay down and leverage our privilege for the sake of the underprivileged, we are joining with Christ in his work of redeeming humanity. It is in this that we share in the life of Christ in our current lives. We, born in privilege, choose to follow the path of Christ by laying down our privilege. We die to ourselves and are able to transcend the cultural expectations placed on us and live to the kingdom values. In humility, we acknowledge our responsibility for the sin in the world and we pick up our cross and follow Jesus; allowing the sins of the world to once again be nailed to the cross in our lives – unraveling the Cycle of Violence. And in this laying down of every aspect of our life, we are also leveraging it for the sake of the underprivileged. As we walk in Christ's footsteps and allow his breath (Spirit) to flow through us, our eyes become transformed into his and we start to see the world and humanity from God's perspective. We see human life become the sacred place of worship from which we are able to serve and worship Christ. Every human becomes one who is worthy of dignity and respect regardless of their differences from us. In this, the body of Christ becomes living and active and once again proclaims, *The Spirit of the Lord is on us, because he has anointed us to proclaim good news to the poor. He has sent us to proclaim freedom for the prisoners and recovery of sight for the blind, to set the oppressed free.*[1]

In following the path of Christ, we find redemption for our personal lives as well as redemption for the world. Redemption that comes through seeing Christ and his image magnified (glorified). When people come up and ask us, "are you the body of Christ?" could our response be the same as Jesus'? *The blind receive sight, the lame walk, those who have leprosy are cleansed, the deaf hear, the dead are raised, and the good news is proclaimed to the poor.*[2] Could it be that this is the reality he has called us to?

Surely, the church *is* called to these characterizations more than any other. The church is called beyond our comfy chairs, great music, organic coffee, and hip pastors. Those are the things that often come to mind when we imagine a church service, but those things aren't the church. Those things aren't the gospel. Sure, we can keep those things, but we can't keep letting them get in the way of the gospel breaking into our lives.

We should consider these things: Let's have a church service in Spanish. Let's have an interpreter. Let's keep the old carpet and instead create a fund for adopting orphans. Let's go to the places no one wants to go because they are too dangerous, "gross," or uncomfortable. Let's pray boldly for miracles. And, in some ways, let's risk getting taken advantage of for the sake of people experiencing love. Was not Jesus treated unfairly and taken advantage of? He was killed! So, let's allow people steal our toilet paper, eat our snacks, dirty our carpet, and stink up our sanctuary if that's what it takes to love the vulnerable. Let's give without asking or policing. To be sure, we should act wisely, but I am all about being radically generous – or, dare I say, *recklessly* loving. It's time we stop assuming that we keep our resources and spend them on ourselves when we should assume to give and spend our resources on others. It's time we stop hoarding out of fear but giving out of the abundance God has given us.

This is the beautiful picture God paints for his Church. Let it be so now. This is a redemption that transforms individuals, societies, and humanity. A redemption that is *making all things new.*[3] A redemption that is occurring in this very moment and that Jesus is inviting us to partake in. Come, let us follow Christ together in seeing this world made new. Let us look forward to the day when we will join with Christ in resurrection and see this work come to completion.

Redeeming Culture

Created to be Cultural

Culture* centers itself around a set of core values that often takes the rightful place of Christ in our lives. These values might include happiness, nation, religiosity, family, security, power, peace, respect, hospitality, creativity, and anything else you might think of. These values determine how people spend their time and other resources. These values also determine how one sees the world and interprets their surroundings.

─────────────────────────────

* In this chapter, I am referring to *culture* in a very broad sense of the word. *Culture* as a "way of living" or a "way of being" or a "way of seeing." We each have our own culture that guides how we live and how we see the world.

Culture is often a source of pride and division (as exemplified in our discussion on "nationalism"). We need to move on from such primitive forms of culture and find our cultural identity as citizens of God's kingdom. However, this does not mean we act like tourists just passing through this world; it means that we are citizens bringing the culture of heaven with us as if we were *ambassadors of Christ*.[4] This does not mean that we reject the earthly culture we were born into. As any good ambassador does, we immerse ourselves in the world and even love the culture we live in; all the while, advancing the priorities of heaven – which is, ultimately, love.

In the church, we are often tempted to reject earthly culture and, thus, create a very boring and ethereal image of who God is. The very nature of humanity is that when people live together, some type of culture will form. We are in a sense, "cultural beings." Therefore, to reject culture is to reject humanity as God created it. Sure, there are certain things within culture that can be wrong, but that is why we talk about "redeeming culture" - not rejecting it.

For example, throughout this book I have emphasized how material possessions are highly valued in the Privileged World. God can redeem this by changing our values about possessions and allow us to use our wealth to be a blessing to the world. Or, for example, America has had a strong historical culture of religious freedom and valuing America as a place where all people can come together as one. The traditional motto of the US is *"E Pluribus Unum"* - "out of many, one." By embracing this already existent cultural value, God can purposefully create one of the most diverse church bodies in the world; thus, glorifying God in a new way that some churches around the world will only experience when the kingdom arrives in its fullness. Similarly, God can take the values of any culture and use them for his purposes - although, this might also include rejecting some of the values of one's culture.

Further, I believe that he placed each person on this earth in a specific place for a reason. I cannot know why God does all he does, but I think one reason is that he intends for each individual to develop in certain way. In fact, the culture we grow up in forms so much of who we are that we might be very different people if we were born into another living situation or another culture. As a result, culture becomes a large part of an individual's identity. Perhaps that is why cultural minorities often will struggle with their identity because they are living in a world of two cultures; they must code-switch between the two constantly. Such experience makes them more adept at seeing the world from multiple perspectives but makes it more difficult to find an identity in a single culture. Jesus provides a home for all cultures and he provides a home for those who don't have a particular cultural identity because he transcends all cultures.

In a sense, we have already discussed how culture plays a role in the church, and how God can be glorified when many cultures come together. I have discussed a vision for a church that embraces diversity, despite its many challenges, for the glory of God. It really is a beautiful, biblical thing when all cultures can be unified with God at the center.

Christianity transcends culture, but it does not neglect culture. The church is really the place where all people were made to meet together, and God is glorified *in* their diversity (not despite it). It is one of the only places in society where the rich and poor gather, Black and Brown and White, the genius and the dumb, the young and the old, all people from all walks of life coming together, each equal in the eyes of Christ and in the eyes of one another. [5] A place where the individual is lost in the bigger picture of community. A place where the wholeness of Christ reigns and a place where the image of Christ is revealed. A place for outsiders as well as "normal" people.

Truly the church is a place where the diversity of the human race comes together as in no other place, to help each other become more Christlike together, and to gaze upon Christ together - celebrating the fact that Christ has redeemed our relationship to himself, our relationship to others, and our relationship to creation. "Love and faithfulness meet together; righteousness and peace kiss each other."[6] It is a place where each of our cultures contribute to the massive and majestic image of who Christ is, and it is a place where each individual culture is redeemed by Christ and made to reflect different aspects of who he is.

Each of us also has a unique worldview that is somewhat based in our own cultures. The culture that we have been trained in is the lens through which we see the world. On a practical level, embracing many cultures allows the church, not just to create a more holistic image of God, but also allows the church to have a more holistic/realistic view of the world. When we embrace different cultures, we learn to embrace different ways of seeing the world; for instance, taking the lens off our eyes and allowing us to see the world through one another's eyes. This is, in reality, one of the things Jesus intended when he saved us. He intended for us to take off the lenses through which we see the world and see it in a new way. This is accomplished through the work of the Holy Spirit amidst a diverse community centered around Christ. The Holy Spirit "lifts the veil" from our eyes that we may more accurately see God[7] and, therefore, more accurately see our neighbor as Christ would.

When it is the Holy Spirit at work, it is not "either God works through the Holy Spirit or he works through people;" it is both. God works through his Spirit in the individualistic you and collectivistic we. This is God's way of working in us to transform the way we see the world. When we become more like Christ, the barriers of language, culture, and fear are swallowed up by Christlike humility - humility that entails a certain ability to endure awkwardness with a patience, a willingness to meet the other person where they are at, and a vision that sees other's as better than oneself.

Suffering as the Path to Cultural Redemption

The world is supposed to *know we are Christians by our love*.[8] I think this means that there is supposed to be a certain Christlike culture radiating from within the church. A culture not defined by popular culture or the like, but a culture defined by the real love of Christ. This culture is supposed to seep out into the world and redeem it. Truly, the church has the potential not just to create personal change but has the power to create profound cultural and social change. In fact, the body of Christ is supposed to use its God-endowed, self-sacrificial, humble authority to create cultural change. Not in a "culture warrior" sense, but in more of a compassionate "culture peacemaker" sense.

For, Jesus profoundly changed world culture with his arrival. Christ challenged every culture when he came to earth. Not rejecting culture but *challenging* it. And this challenge has the potential to transform culture in a radical way. But, when culture is challenged, there will be pushback and it will necessarily result in the suffering of Christ's body. Martin Luther King Jr. understood this deeply. In his famous *Letter from Birmingham Jail*, he pleaded with his fellow believers to use the authority that God had given the church in order to work for justice. In one part, he wrote:

> There was a time when the church was very powerful. It was during that period that the early Christians rejoiced when they were deemed worthy to suffer for what they believed. In those days, the church was not merely a thermometer that recorded the ideas and principles of popular opinion; it was the thermostat that transformed the mores of society. Wherever the early Christians entered a town the power structure got disturbed and immediately sought to convict them for being "disturbers of the peace" and "outside agitators." But they went on with the conviction that they were "a colony of heaven" and had to obey God rather than man. They were small in number but big in commitment. They were too God-intoxicated to be "astronomically intimidated." They brought an end to such ancient evils as infanticide and gladiatorial contest.

In this context, he was pleading with his fellow believers to join the cause of justice and fight for the oppressed and persecuted in America. Nevertheless, this letter applies to the church for all time. In this quote, MLK links the suffering of the Church with the authority of the Church, and the authority of the church with the ability to bring about cultural and social change. But, this isn't a suffering for the sake of suffering, it is a suffering for the sake of justice. It is the "common suffering" compassion that brings about change, and this common suffering is always the mark of Christlike love. Christlike love is not without compassion. This is a type of laying and leveraging of our privilege to "speak truth to power." In our nonviolent turning-of-the-cheek resistance, we radically lay down our rights for the sake of the oppressed.

Considering this, I do not think it a coincidence that at a moment when the privileged church enjoys unprecedented freedom and prosperity it continually has lessening authority and cultural influence. Instead of being a thermostat, the church has become a thermometer that measures the popular culture of society.

As a result, Kenneth Bailey emphasizes, "The message of the gospel is in danger of being compromised by the value system that supports its culture and its goals."[9] The culture of the world around us seeps into the church and saturates it so much so that its values and ideals are the same as that of the world. Or worse still, it becomes defined by fear of the culture at large and, therefore, seeks to always bad-talk the "world's culture;" all the while, compromising the gospel in order to fit in with the mainstream culture.

Church services turn into entertainment avenues instead of places where volunteers gather to serve. The word "service" should entail that there is some sort of "serving" going on in the church. But it has become a place where people go to church to be served rather than to serve. The church often ensures that self-help courses are taught to ensure that Christians are happy, healthy, and wealthy. All the while, their money is rotting in their banks, when they could be put into the eternal investment that comes from caring for the least of these. The church embraces *Love* as the central theme, but neglects "common suffering" as an essential component of this love. The church has lost its authority because it has lost its grit that once possessed the people of the early church whose allegiance was only to the kingdom of heaven. If the American church wishes to see true cultural change, even global change, it is going to have to take a sense of love, mixed with a willingness to suffer, and an active laying down one's life for godly living. Then, the world will see Christ, and culture will be redeemed in its beholding of him.

If we wish to walk the path of Jesus and see the world redeemed, we must seek a fundamental worldview shift that brings us in line with Jesus. The average person in the church must acknowledge the real cost of discipleship and all its life-altering consequences; and church leadership must stop preaching a watered-down gospel that is easier for the privileged to stomach. Maybe then, we can get our heads out of the clouds and walk this sacred ground with humility and authority as opposed to walking with pride and ignorance.

Redeeming Humanity

We must not get caught up in the fallen thinking *that the redemption and salvation of the world falls on us.* Such thinking will only make us shrivel up in hopelessness or puff us up with pride. Ultimately, salvation hinges on the action of Jesus Christ and his Spirit.[10] The action of Jesus on the cross and the action of the Holy Spirit in our lives. And, if we get to partake in those actions, it is only by God's grace lavished upon us. And, in God's grace, we do partake in those actions by carrying our own crosses and allowing the Spirit to work through us in the lives of others.

However, our culture of privilege has watered down this beautiful picture of salvation into a passive acceptance of righteousness from God - all one must do is "pray a prayer" without much fundamentally changing. The "righteous change" that is usually expected when one becomes a Christian is that they are to now "sin less" than they did before. To Jesus, such righteousness is not righteousness at all. Righteousness is when someone is "made right with God" and now is a part of God's plan for humanity. Yet, we cannot join God's plan through legalistically trying to follow the law and commands of Christ. In this way, we might think we partake in God's plan by obeying the law, chopping off one's hands when they sin, and by selling all they have and giving it to the poor. God's plan isn't that we would *act righteously* but that we would *be righteous* to our core; and in being righteous, we will naturally act in the way God desires.

Through the work of Christ, we are made righteous and we are enabled to act righteously; therefore, our righteous acts become evidence of our righteous condition that Jesus has granted us. But, our righteous condition cannot be obtained through such righteous acts. It is a fine, but important distinction.

Again, our righteous acts are not just a cessation of sinful actions but a participation in the saving acts of Christ and his Holy Spirit in the world. The biblical Greek and

Hebrew words for *righteousness* can also be translated as *justice*. Righteousness and justice are one and the same. We have become focused on *righteousness* as meaning legalistic, moral behavior and have lost the fact that the biblical word for *righteousness* also means *justice*. And *justice*, in the biblical sense, means a lifting up of the oppressed and downtrodden. *Righteousness* does not mean mere "moral purity" (as I was brought up to believe) but is defined by our right relationship with God and neighbor. Therefore, true righteous behavior becomes a laying down and leveraging of our privilege for the sake of the underprivileged. We partake in the acts of Jesus when we embrace righteous justice as his will for our lives, we partake in bringing the *saving acts* of Jesus and his Holy Spirit into the lives of those around us.[*]

Therefore, the church should be very concerned with social justice issues (or *social righteousness* issues).[†] We seek to show compassion and bring about change that will result in kingdom conditions. Conditions where God's will is carried out *on earth as it is in heaven.*[11] And, in such conditions, the presence and knowledge of God will be much more accessible to the average individual.

---

[*] Perhaps, next time you read the Bible, whenever you come across the word *righteousness*, read it again with the word *justice* in its place. By doing so, I have come to see the message of Christ with fresh eyes and feel I have gained a deeper and more Biblical view of what righteousness and justice mean – and maybe you will as well.

[†] To be clear, we don't participate in social justice activism as much of the world does - which is often marked by the emotions of anger, resentment, fear, and revenge. It must be done in a manner worthy of gospel - marked by love, forgiveness, grace, peace, patience, and mercy (the fruit of the Spirit).

Christianity: An Utterly Human Faith

I have been realizing how utterly *human* life is. Throughout my life, I have had a longing for "mystical experiences" or to experience the Holy Spirit in a way that is completely "out of this world." I have wanted more of the "supernatural;" but, for the most part, it has been *all too human.* I wish to walk into the sanctuary and completely feel the "thickness" of the Spirit in the air. I believe such desires are good and noble and come from a heart that desires more of God, and, indeed, we should long for such experiences as these can have a formative impact on our lives. Although God does work in the mystical and spiritual, God seems to largely work through the incredibly human, earthy, and humble things of this life to portray his majesty.

Maybe God intends for the "human experience" to be a mostly human experience. That's why God became a human for us to know him, instead of simply revealing himself in a miraculous vision. *The Christian's life is to be utterly human.* If this is the case, I think that many churches have it slightly wrong. So many of us focus so much on the "experiences" or, even more shallowly, hype up our emotions and feelings in an attempt to feel something spiritual or gain connection with God; all the while, God is most commonly experienced in the most human of circumstances.

Christ and the Spirit is experienced in the love of a sister or brother that drops everything to spend his day with you when you are having a difficult day; in the eyes of a Father who is proud of his son for absolutely no reason; in the cleaning and changing the diaper for an adult with special needs; in the doing of dishes for your neighbor; in the sun coming through the trees in the forest; in the making of a meal for the homeless; in the everyday interactions with others; in the everyday community we spend with other

believers; in the conversations we have with one another; in
the goodbyes that we say; and in the greetings we say. For
the Christian, Christ saturates such human activities. It is
in the tears, in the joys, in the monotone. It is the everyday,
human experiences, that are the most mundane, beautiful,
sacred, and God revealing. God is under the surface,
working in and through us humans in mystical and mind-
blowing ways. We will look back and say, "Surely, God was
among us when we were together." We will understand that
many conversations, laughs, walks, glances, and human
experiences were all pointing to God. All the moments
spent in the humble service of others was time spent serving
Christ. The human experience and the "spiritual
experience" are brought together into unity through Christ.
And, to think, this is only a glimpse of the kingdom that is
to come in Christ.

Next time you are discouraged that you haven't
"experienced God lately," and you've been crying out for a
mystical experience, or a feeling of God's nearness, or
maybe even a vision of him, perhaps it's because you haven't
been serving him or spending time with other believers in
communion. Consider that God primarily works through
humans and that maybe you just need to spend some time
with humans. If you don't feel close to God, perhaps, find
the homeless man on the street, or call up the friend you
know is lonely, or give a drink to the thirsty, and spend
some time loving in the name of Jesus. When you love in
his name, you are loving him, and you cannot be far from
him when you are loving him. Be comforted in that.

On the other hand, if you're burned out from pouring into people and are having difficulty seeing Christ in others or difficulty having the patience to treat them as Christ would, perhaps what you need to do is get away and spend some time in prayer, reading your bible, reorienting your mind and thoughts so that Christ can give you renewed life to continue to love like he has loved you. Spend some time listening to him and listening in silence as you breathe in the Spirit of God. Lose yourself in worship – whether that be on your knees in your closet or with your hands raised to music in the sanctuary.

Prayer and action are inextricably linked. And if you have been all action without any centering prayer, it is no wonder your life is off balance. Similarly, if you have been all prayer and no action, it may be no wonder that prayer has become stale and feels empty of Jesus.

Even still, we will never be satisfied in this life. The present state of humanity is one that has not yet been brought to complete new creation.

> "I consider that our present sufferings are not worth comparing with the glory that will be revealed in us. For the creation waits in eager expectation for the children of God to be revealed. For the creation was subjected to frustration, not by its own choice, but by the will of the one who subjected it, in hope that the creation itself will be liberated from its bondage to decay and brought into the freedom and glory of the children of God.
>
> "We know that the whole creation has been groaning as in the pains of childbirth right up to the

present time. Not only so, but we ourselves, who have the firstfruits of the Spirit, groan inwardly as we wait eagerly for our adoption to sonship, the redemption of our bodies. For in this hope, we were saved. But hope that is seen is no hope at all. Who hopes for what they already have? But if we hope for what we do not yet have, we wait for it patiently.

"In the same way, the Spirit helps us in our weakness. We do not know what we ought to pray for, but the Spirit himself intercedes for us through wordless groans. And he who searches our hearts knows the mind of the Spirit, because the Spirit intercedes for God's people in accordance with the will of God. And we know that in all things God works for the good of those who love him, who have been called according to his purpose. For those God foreknew he also predestined to be conformed to the image of his Son, that he might be the firstborn among many brothers and sisters. And those he predestined, he also called; those he called, he also justified; those he justified, he also glorified." (Romans 8:18-30))

Brothers and Sisters, the Christian life is surely something to look forward to. But, even more so, the resurrection into new creation is something that we long for with all our being. In the meantime, we groan and pray that the world might see God for who he is. In the meantime, we make our home on earth, just as Jesus made his home on earth. Yet, this does not mean we become attached to this earth. Many have become so attached to the earth that they become deluded and trade the new creation for a pittance. We now, become like Jesus in that our home is equally in heaven and on earth.[12] Even still, we are like *alien strangers of this world;*[13] *like soldiers, and must not become entangled in civilian life and such attachments.*[14] Therefore, we

make our home here and long for the fullness of his
kingdom. For, this world in its present form is passing. We
wait for the day when creation itself will be made new.
When this happens, we will be adopted into God's family
and we will live with him and he will be our God. We will
speak to him as if we are speaking face to face. We eagerly
await full adoption into sonship. Then, we will finally be
home - living in a redeemed heaven and a redeemed earth
that has been brought together in oneness.

The temple is founded into eternity and God's kingdom
reigns. Now, today, the biblical vision of the temple of God
being a place where every nation and every tongue flock to
is becoming a reality in some small scale:

> In the last days
>   the mountain of the Lord's temple
> will be established
>   as the highest of the mountains;
> it will be exalted above the hills,
>   and all nations will stream to it.
>   Many peoples will come and say,
>   "Come, let us go up to the
> mountain of the Lord,
>   to the temple of the God of Jacob.
> He will teach us his ways,
>   so that we may walk in his paths."
> The law will go out from Zion,
>   the word of the Lord from Jerusalem.
> He will judge between the nations
>   and will settle disputes for many
> peoples.
> They will beat their swords into

> plowshares
>   and their spears into pruning hooks.
> Nation will not take up sword against
> nation,
>   nor will they train for war anymore.
>   Isaiah 2:2-4 NIV

This is truly a biblical vision of worship, of which the prophets anticipated. When diverse people come together as one, in worship of Jesus, they are catching a glimpse of the kingdom of heaven – a glimpse of the new creation. We are catching a glimpse of the redeeming work that Jesus started on the cross and is currently bringing to completion. As Christians in the Western world, we are in a unique place to really see the coming together of diverse people as is not seen in the rest of the world. Further, as Christians in the Privileged World, we are in a position of privilege and advantage from which Christ is bidding us to use our advantage to work for the disadvantaged. Not only that, but Jesus is bidding us to come and die to ourselves and find our resurrection in him.

Truly, Jesus reigns today, and we get to be a part of his wonderful work. What a joyous privilege we share in! What grace God has lavished upon us. When the vision of Christ captures our hearts, we join with Christ in the redemption and transformation of this world. When we lay down our lives for the sake of righteous justice, we join with Christ in his work; we glorify and magnify the image of Christ. Our minds and hearts are filled with hope instead of despair and we can truly believe Christ when he proclaims,

Look, I am making all things new.[15]

What a wonder that we get to partake in this new creation! Oh, just to catch a glimpse of this new work! Walk with me as we walk with Christ. Join with me in proclaiming Isaiah 61 as the truth of what Christ is doing within and through us! Let these words seep deep into your soul and let it drench your Christian walk:

> "The Spirit of *Yahweh* is on *us*,
>   because the Lord has anointed *us*
>   to proclaim good news to the poor.
> He has sent *us* to bind up the
> brokenhearted,
>   to proclaim freedom for the captives
>   and release from darkness for the
> prisoners,
> to proclaim the year of the Lord's favor.

Isaiah 61:1-2 NIV
(words in italics modified)

A FINAL WORD

Redemption for the Privileged

Now, I turn it over to you. It is up to *you* to decide what you are going to do about the call of Christ. It is up to you to wrestle with your privileged position in life and to give it all to Christ. It is up to you to faithfully wrestle while understanding that it won't always end with something as simple as "finding the answer." Though, we also must not let our wrestling become an excuse that keeps us from ever doing God's will, there comes a point when we must submit to God and just simply do what he desires.

Will you hear the word God gives you, without qualification?

Woe to the rich, well-fed, happy, and popular.[1] For, it is harder for a rich man to enter the kingdom, than it is for a camel to fit through the eye of the needle.[2] To anyone who is not rich toward God, but stores up things for themselves God will say, 'you fool, I will demand your life from you this very night. What then will you possess?'[3] In your lifetime, you received good things while the poor received bad things; don't be surprised when you are suffering in hell and the poor are comforted by me.[4] The servant who knows his master's will and still does not do what the master

*wants will be beaten with many blows. Everyone who has been
entrusted with much, much will be expected.⁵*

*If you haven't been proven trustworthy in your handling of
worldly wealth, how can you be trusted with true riches in
Heaven?⁶ Do you not know? Those who do not give up everything,
they cannot be my disciples.⁷ So, when you have a dinner party;
invite the poor, the crippled, the lame, the blind - then you will be
blessed.⁸ If you have two shirts, give your extra one to the one who
doesn't have any.⁹ Life is more than food or clothing; seek first the
kingdom and you will be provided for.¹⁰*

Will you put your weight on Christ and enter into the vision
of life that he is inviting you into? Will you lay down your
life for those who are unworthy of it; just as Jesus laid down
his life for you? Will you accept the authority that Christ
has given you to be his hands and feet to the world? Will
you practice the righteous justice Jesus calls you to?

It will not be easy. You might cry to your Father in
heaven to the point of tears and bloody sweat, "Take this
cup from me."¹¹ It'll be like carrying your own cross next
to Jesus; it'll be the death of you and many of your desires.
Yes, count the cost to see if this is something that you really
want.

But it is also the resurrection life of Jesus that you get
in return. It is the life spent with Christ encountered in the
poor and in the community of Christ. It is a life of
reconciliation and redemption. A life rich with the presence
of Christ. A life, who, in the body of Christ, joins into the
building of a new kingdom of shalom. An abundant life.

We are not called to a life of religious duty, nice church
services, and simple moral restraint. Indeed, "he has told
you O mortal, what is good. And what does the LORD

require of you? To act justly and to love mercy and to walk humbly with your God."[12]

> This is the kind of fast day I'm after:
>> to break the chains of injustice,
>> get rid of exploitation in the workplace,
>> free the oppressed,
>> cancel debts.
> What I'm interested in seeing you do is:
>> sharing your food with the hungry,
>> inviting the homeless poor into your homes,
>> putting clothes on the shivering ill-clad,
>> being available to your own families.
> Do this and the lights will turn on,
>> and your lives will turn around at once.
> Your righteousness will pave your way.
>> The GOD of glory will secure your passage.
> Then when you pray, GOD will answer.
>> You'll call out for help and I'll say, 'Here I am.'

> If you get rid of unfair practices,
>> quit blaming victims,
>> quit gossiping about other people's sins,
> If you are generous with the hungry
>> and start giving yourselves to the down-and-out,
> Your lives will begin to glow in the darkness,
>> your shadowed lives will be bathed in sunlight.
> I will always show you where to go.
>> I'll give you a full life in the emptiest of places—

firm muscles, strong bones.
You'll be like a well-watered garden,
a gurgling spring that never runs dry.
You'll use the old rubble of past lives to build
anew,
rebuild the foundations from out of your
past.
You'll be known as those who can fix anything,
restore old ruins, rebuild and renovate,
make the community livable again."

- Isaiah 58:6-9 MSG

REFERENCES

Prologue
[1] Matthew 5:48
[2] Genesis 32:22-32
[3] Matthew 19:24

Chapter 1: Gospel for the Privileged
[1] World Bank (2008) as cited by http://www.globalrichlist.com/
[2] Psalm 40, 70, 86, 109, 113, to name a few
[3] Luke 4:18-19 NIV
[4] Phillip Jenkins, *The Next Christendom* (New York, NY: Oxford University Press, 2007) 215
[5] Mark 10:24-27
[6] John 10:18 NIV, NLT
[7] Luke 4:22 NIV
[8] Mark 10:20-22 NIV
[9] Matthew 6:21
[10] Luke 6:24-26
[11] Matthew 12:34
[12] John 8:44
[13] Matthew 19:21
[14] Luke 19:8; Then there's Levi (aka Matthew) doing similar and leaving his profession to follow Jesus (Mark 2:16).
[15] Isaiah 58:2 NIV Isaiah 58:2 NIV
[16] Isaiah 58:6-7 NIV Isaiah 58:6-7 NIV
[17] Phillip Jenkins, *The Next Christendom* (New York, NY: Oxford University Press, 2007) 148
[18] Revelations 3:15-17 NIV
[19] Galatians 2:20 NIV

Chapter 2: The Image of God
[1] Genesis 1:26 NLT
[2] A.W. Tozer, *Jesus,* (Chicago, IL: Moody Publishers, 2017)
[3] Genesis 1:31 NIV
[4] Genesis 3:4
[5] Hosea 6:6
[6] 1 Samuel 15:22

[7] Proverbs 21:3
[8] Isaiah 1:11
[9] Micah 6:8 ESV
[10] Colossians 1:15 NLT
[11] Psalm 51:5
[12] Job 9:32-35
[13] Luke 3:38
[14] Romans 5
[15] John 10:10
[16] A.W. Tozer, *Jesus* (Chicago, IL: Moody Publishers, 2017), 60
[17] N.T Wright, *Simply Jesus* (New York, NY: HarperOne, 2011) 185
[18] Exodus 19:6 NIV
[19] 1 Peter 2:24 NLT
[20] 2 Corinthians 5:21 NIV
[21] 1 Corinthians 1:18 NLT
[22] Galatians 6:2
[23] 1 Corinthians 15:19 paraphrase
[24] Colossians 1:18
[25] CS Lewis, *The Last Battle* (New York, NY: Macmillan, 1956)
[26] CS Lewis, *The Great Divorce*, (New York, NY : The Macmillan Company, 1946)
[27] 1 Corinthians 13:21 NLT
[28] Luke 24:31
[29] Luke 24:36
[30] Wording borrowed from N.T. Wright and Gustavo Gutierrez
[31] Romans 8:18-30 NIV
[32] Daniel 7
[33] Acts 7:6 NIV
[34] All Sons and Daughters, "Great are you Lord" (Integrity Music, 2013) [Song]
[35] John 16:7 ESV
[36] A.W. Tozer, *Jesus* (Chicago, IL: Moody Publishers, 2017), 65
[37] John 16:7
[38] Matthew 13:17
[39] Acts 2:17
[40] 2 Corinthians 3:18 ESV
[41] Galatians 2:20
[42] 2 Corinthians 5:17
[43] Genesis 2:23

Chapter 3: Humility and Authority

[1] Philippians 2:12-13 NIV
[2] Genesis 1:26
[3] Psalm 138:6
[4] James 4:6; Proverbs 3:34
[5] Proverbs 16:18
[6] Daniel 4:27
[7] Matthew 16:25
[8] Matthew 19:29
[9] Paragraph themes taken from a Loren Cunningham talk entitled "relinquishing our rights."
[10] Matthew 26:52
[11] Matthew 5:39 NIV
[12] Matthew 5:13-14
[13] Proverbs 31:8 NIV
[14] Luke 6:29-30
[15] Matthew 5:39-42
[16] John 10:16-17 NIV
[17] John 15: 13 NIV
[18] Ephesians 3:1
[19] Luke 14:28
[20] Luke 9:23 NIV
[21] Dietrich Bonhoeffer, *The Cost of Discipleship*, (New York, NY: Macmillan, 1959)
[22] Luke 9:24
[23] Romans 8:18 NIV
[24] Paraphrase of Dietrich Bonhoeffer's last words before his execution
[25] 1 Corinthians 1:18 NIV
[26] 1 Corinthians 1:18-19
[27] 2 Corinthians 2:16 NLT
[28] Luke 16:10
[29] Galatians 6:2
[30] 1 Timothy 1:15 NIV
[31] Luke 18:14
[32] Fyodor Dostoyevsky, *The Brothers Karamazov*, (New York, NY: Vintage books, 1950) Chapter 3
[33] Matthew 20:22-23

[34] G.K. Chesterton, *Orthodoxy* (Garden City, N.Y.: Doubleday, 1959), 41

[35] 1 Corinthians 12:26 NIV

[36] Daniel 9:3-16 ESV

[37] Fernando Meirelles (Director). (2019). *The Two Popes.* Netflix

[38] 1 Corinthians 3:7

[39] Matthew 5:3 NIV

[40] Proverbs 18:12

[41] Philippians 2:9-11 NLT Philippians 2:9-11 NLT

[42] 1 John 3:2 NIV

[43] C.S. Lewis, *Mere Christianity* (1952; Harper Collins: 2001) 59

[44] Genesis 1:26 NIV

[45] Matthew 28:18 NIV

[46] John 13:1-17

[47] John 13:13 NIV

[48] Mark 12:43-44

[49] Matthew 25:14-30

[50] Matthew 25:31-46

[51] Matthew 13:45-46

[52] Matthew 6:19-21

[53] Martin Luther King Jr, *Letter From Birmingham Jail,* (San Francisco, CA: Harper San Francisco, 1994)

[54] 2 Timothy 3:12

[55] Acts 5:41 NIV

[56] Edward Gilbreath, *Birmingham Revolution* (Downers Grove, IL: InterVarsity Press, 2013) 55

[57] Girardi, "Amore Cristiano e violenza rivoluzionalia," *Viollenza dei cristiani.* (as quoted in *A Theology of Liberation: History, Politics, and Salvation,* (Maryknoll, NY: Orbis Books, 1973). *p 276*

Chapter 4: The Global Christian

[1] Ravi Zacharias, *Jesus Among Other Gods* (Nashville, TN: Word Publishing, 2000) 43

[2] John 4:46 NIV

[3] John 7:52 NIV and NLT

[4] Galatians 3:28

[5] 1 Peter 2:9

[6] Eric Ludy, *Depraved Indifference,* (Bravehearted Christian Productions, 2010) https://www.youtube.com/watch?v=UWHJ6-YhSYQ

7 Matthew 10:42
8 2 Corinthians 9:1-5
9 Galatians 6:2
10 Matthew 19:24
11 Luke 6:24
12 Matthew 5:3
13 A.W. Tozer, *Jesus* (Chicago, IL: Moody Publishers, 2017), 157
14 Matthew 19:21 NIV
15 Luke 14:33 NIV; ESV; NASB
16 Luke 3:11
17 Matthew 8:20
18 Matthew 23:26; Luke 11:39
19 Matthew 23:26; Luke 11:39
20 Galatians 5:14
21 Matthew 6:25-27
22 James Keenan, *Moral Wisdom: Lessons and Texts from the Catholic Tradition.* (London, UK: Sheed & Ward, 2004)
23 Luke 10:29
24 Gustavo Gutierrez, *A Theology of Liberation: History, Politics, and Salvation,* (Maryknoll, NY: Orbis Books, 1973). *p.* 198
25 Romans 12:2
26 2 Peter 1:3
27 Matthew 25:23
28 Matthew 7:21-23
29 Matthew 7:14
30 Francis and Lisa Chan, *Watermark Marriage Ministry Conference,* (Crazy Love, 2015) https://www.youtube.com/watch?v=SgWk5Bsy9es
31 Genesis 1:28 NIV
32 Matthew 28:19
33 Romans 8:34
34 Matthew 6:33
35 James 2:16
36 Nehemiah 1-2
37 Nehemiah 4:9
38 James 2:20 NKJV
39 James 2:14-17 NIV
40 To adapt the Cornel West quote: "justice is what love looks like in public"

Chapter 5: Humanity in Perspective
1 John 3:30
2 1 John 3:2
3 John 2:15
4 Matthew 26:11
5 Matthew 11:11
6 Luke 3:16; John 1:27
7 Matthew 20:28
8 Matthew 25:40
9 Isaiah 53:2-3 NIV
10 Gustavo Gutierrez, *A Theology of Liberation: History, Politics, and Salvation*, (Maryknoll, NY: Orbis Books, 1973). p 201
11 Matthew 22:37-39 NIV
12 Galatians 5:22-23
13 NT Wright, *Simply Jesus*, (New York, NY: HarperOne, 2011) p. 132
14 1 Corinthians 6:19
15 John 4:23-24 NIV
16 Psalm 84:1
17 Matthew 18:20 NIV
18 Isaiah 56:7
19 Matthew 25:40
20 Keith Green, "Open Your Eyes," (Sparrow, 1990)
21 Romans 8:20-21
22 Dietrich Bonhoeffer quoted in Eric Metaxas, *Bonhoeffer* (Thomas Nelson, 2010), p. 456
23 Luke 17:21
24 Philippians 3:21
25 2 Corinthians 5:1 NLT
26 CS Lewis, *The Last Battle*, (New York, NY: Macmillan, 1956)
27 2 Corinthians 5:4
28 Jon Walker, *Costly Grace*, (Abilene, TX: Leafwood Publishers, 2010) 72
29 Ephesians 6:12 NIV
30 Gustavo Gutierrez, *A Theology of Liberation: History, Politics, and Salvation*, (Maryknoll, NY: Orbis Books, 1973). p 231
31 Wolfhart Pannenberg as quoted in Gustavo Gutierrez, *A Theology of Liberation: History, Politics, and Salvation*, (Maryknoll, NY: Orbis Books, 1973). p. 231

[32] Gustavo Gutierrez, *A Theology of Liberation: History, Politics, and Salvation*, (Maryknoll, NY: Orbis Books, 1973). p 199

Chapter 6: Embrace of Diversity
[1] Gustavo Gutierrez, *A Theology of Liberation: History, Politics, and Salvation*, (Maryknoll, NY: Orbis Books, 1973). 11y
[2] Genesis 2:18
[3] Genesis 1:27
[4] Genesis 1:26
[5] John 17:21
[6] Ephesians 5:31
[7] Dean Sherman, *Relationships: The Key to Love, Sex, and Everything Else*, (Seattle, WA: YWAM Publishing, 2002) 19
[8] Martin Luther King Jr., *Where Do We Go from Here: Chaos or Community* (New York, NY: Harper & Row, 1967)
[9] Phillip Jenkins, *The Next Christendom* (New York, NY: Oxford University Press, 2007) 3
[10] Matthew 5:44
[11] Martin Luther King Jr, *Letter From Birmingham Jail*, (San Francisco, CA: Harper San Francisco, 1994)
[12] John 13:35
[13] 1 Corinthians 13:4
[14] David A. Anderson, *Gracism* (Downers Grove, IL: InterVarsity Press, 2007)
[15] Luke 22:14–20
[16] 1 Corinthians 11:17-22; 27-29
[17] Gustavo Gutierrez, *A Theology of Liberation: History, Politics, and Salvation*, (Maryknoll, NY: Orbis Books, 1973). 262

Chapter 7: Difficulty with Diversity
[1] Gustavo Gutierrez, *A Theology of Liberation: History, Politics, and Salvation*, (Maryknoll, NY: Orbis Books, 1973). 138
[2] Titus 3:8-10 ESV
[3] Acts 7:3
[4] Galatians 5:6 ESV
[5] 1 Timothy 3:15 NIV
[6] Galatians 5:6 NIV
[7] James 2:13
[8] Romans 15:1
[9] i.e., Matthew 15:12

[10] Genesis 2:16-17 NIV
[11] Greg Boyd, *Repenting of Religion* (Grand Rapids, MI: Baker Books, 2004)
[12] Matthew 7:1
[13] Dallas Willard, *The Divine Conspiracy* (San Francisco, CA: HarperSanFrancisco, 1998) 35
[14] Luke 19:7
[15] Luke 7:39
[16] paraphrase of multiple quotes of Jesus – Luke 7:47; Matthew 13:33
[17] Matthew 9:36
[18] John 5:14; John 8:11
[19] Luke 19:8
[20] John 4:4-26
[21] John 8:7
[22] Matthew 13:24-30

Chapter 8: Redeeming Humanity
[1] Luke 4:18 NIV
[2] Matthew 11:5 NIV
[3] Revelation 21:5
[44] 2 Corinthians 5:20
[5] Steve Turner, *Imagine* (Downers Grove, IL: InterVarsity Press, 2001) 122
[6] Psalm 85:10 NIV
[7] 2 Corinthians 3:16
[8] John 13:35
[9] Kenneth Bailey, *Jesus Through Middle Eastern Eyes* (Downers Grove, IL: InterVarsity Press, 2008) 166
[10] Gustavo Gutierrez, *A Theology of Liberation: History, Politics, and Salvation*, (Maryknoll, NY: Orbis Books, 1973). 256
[11] Matthew 6:10
[12] Ephesians 1:10
[13] 1 Peter 2:11
[14] 2 Timothy 2:4
[15] Revelation 21:5

A Final Word
[1] Luke 6:24-26
[2] Luke 18:25

3 Luke 12:20-21
4 Luke 16:19-31
5 Luke 12:47-48
6 Luke 16:11
7 Luke 14:33 NIV
8 Luke 14:13-14
9 Luke 3:11
10 Luke 12:22-33 NIV
11 Luke 22:44
12 Micah 6:8 NIV

Made in the USA
Monee, IL
17 May 2021

68748380R00144